MORE

FABULUS FLWERS

Mini-Quilts in Dimensional Appliqué

SHARON K BAKER

Martingale®
& COMPANY

Dedication

I would like to thank my family for always believing in me and for understanding when things get out of control with my obsessive behavior. And I would like to thank Martingale & Company for taking a chance on me a second time. I am grateful for all the good things and good people in my life.

Credits

President & CEO • Tom Wierzbicki

Publisher • Jane Hamada

Editorial Director • Mary V. Green

Managing Editor • Tina Cook

Technical Editor • Laurie Baker

Copy Editor • Melissa Bryan

Design Director • Stan Green

Production Manager • Regina Girard

Illustrator • Laurel Strand

Cover & Text Designer • Shelly Garrison

Photographer • Brent Kane

Mission Statement

Dedicated to providing quality products and service to inspire creativity.

More Fabulous Flowers:
Mini-Quilts in Dimensional Appliqué
© 2008 by Sharon K Baker

That Patchwork Place®
is an imprint of Martingale & Company®.

Martingale & Company
20205 144th Ave. NE
Woodinville, WA 98072-8478 USA
www.martingale-pub.com

Printed in China
13 12 11 10 09   8 7 6 5 4 3

Library of Congress Cataloging-in-Publication Data
Library of Congress Control Number: 2008012250

ISBN: 978-1-56477-819-2

CONTENTS

INTRODUCTION

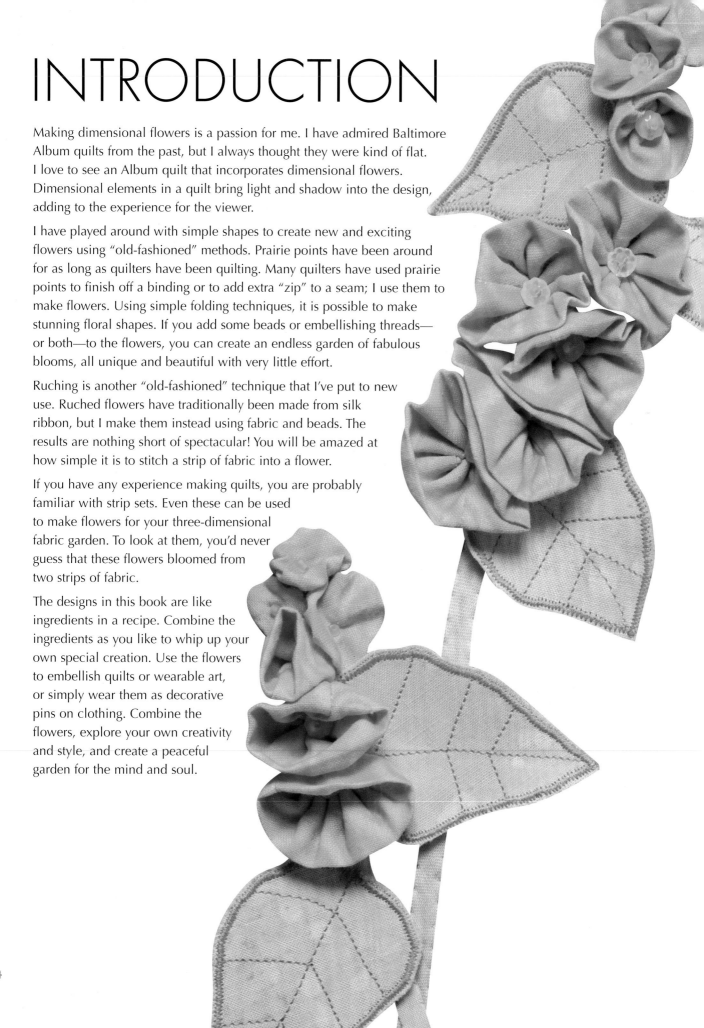

Making dimensional flowers is a passion for me. I have admired Baltimore Album quilts from the past, but I always thought they were kind of flat. I love to see an Album quilt that incorporates dimensional flowers. Dimensional elements in a quilt bring light and shadow into the design, adding to the experience for the viewer.

I have played around with simple shapes to create new and exciting flowers using "old-fashioned" methods. Prairie points have been around for as long as quilters have been quilting. Many quilters have used prairie points to finish off a binding or to add extra "zip" to a seam; I use them to make flowers. Using simple folding techniques, it is possible to make stunning floral shapes. If you add some beads or embellishing threads— or both—to the flowers, you can create an endless garden of fabulous blooms, all unique and beautiful with very little effort.

Ruching is another "old-fashioned" technique that I've put to new use. Ruched flowers have traditionally been made from silk ribbon, but I make them instead using fabric and beads. The results are nothing short of spectacular! You will be amazed at how simple it is to stitch a strip of fabric into a flower.

If you have any experience making quilts, you are probably familiar with strip sets. Even these can be used to make flowers for your three-dimensional fabric garden. To look at them, you'd never guess that these flowers bloomed from two strips of fabric.

The designs in this book are like ingredients in a recipe. Combine the ingredients as you like to whip up your own special creation. Use the flowers to embellish quilts or wearable art, or simply wear them as decorative pins on clothing. Combine the flowers, explore your own creativity and style, and create a peaceful garden for the mind and soul.

TOOLS and SUPPLIES

The following supplies were used to make the projects in this book, although you won't need all of them for every project; check the materials list with each project for the specific supplies required for that quilt.

Fabric: I prefer hand-dyed or batik fabrics because of the wonderful shading in the colors. I don't wash my fabrics before I use them because I like the crispness of a new fabric, but I do test for colorfastness. Snip off a small piece of fabric and place it in hot water. If you see any dye in the water, wash the entire piece of fabric until the water runs clear.

Batting: Use cotton or polyester batting. Because these quilts are small, they do not take much batting; a crib-size piece of batting can be cut into small pieces as needed, or a long-arm machine quilter may be willing to give you scraps.

Beads: Beads can be found in craft stores, bead shops, and from online sources. Avoid plastic and metal beads because they may discolor the fabric over time.

Hand-sewing needles: I use size 12 needles known as Betweens for all my hand-sewing needs. Because they are short and strong, they can be pushed through thick layers of fabric.

Machine-sewing needles: I use size 70/10 Microtex needles for machine piecing. They have a fine shaft and a sharp point and are perfect for sewing densely woven batik fabrics. Use a quilting needle for quilting the background fabric of a quilt.

Machine-piecing thread: Cotton thread works best, although you can use cotton-wrapped polyester. Use 50-weight thread for all piecing and hand stitching.

Quilting and topstitching threads: Thread manufacturers assign numbers to thread weights; the larger the number, the finer the thread. Topstitching threads are usually 35- or 40-weight, quilting threads are usually 40- or 50-weight, machine embroidery thread is usually 60-weight, and silk threads can be as fine as 100-weight. If you want your quilting to show, use a heavier thread; the stitches will sit on the surface of the quilt top more than a finer thread, which tends to sink into the fabric. Play around with different thread weights and types until you find the look you like.

Embellishing threads and yarns: Almost any type of thread or yarn can be used to embellish a quilt. Look for different types of embellishing threads and yarns in craft and needle-art stores.

Bias-tape makers: I use the ¼", ⅜", and ½" tape makers to form perfect stems and vines.

Water-soluble fabric glue: I like to glue-baste the stems and vines to the background fabric and then hand appliqué them in place. Use a needle-tip applicator to apply small dots of glue to the back of the bias-tape stems, and then stick them to the background fabric. Don't apply the glue too thickly or it will be very difficult to push the needle through the edge of the stem.

Embellishing glue: This glue is designed to be strong and flexible, making it perfect for holding beads in place. My favorite brand is Aleene's Jewel-It. It is washable, but cannot be dry-cleaned.

Oil pastel sticks/artist paint sticks: Several of the flowers in this book have accents of added color. To create this effect, I used oil pastel sticks to rub color into the fabric. Look for acid-free oil pastels/paint sticks in the art department of your local craft store. Use a small stencil brush to rub the color into the fabric; blow (don't wipe) away any excess "crumbs" of color off the fabric. The oil in the pastel paint takes about 24 hours to dry, so don't rub the fabric or you will smear it.

Rotary-cutting tools: A 6" x 24" and a 15" square ruler are handy for the projects in this book. Use them with a cutting mat and a rotary cutter with a sharp blade.

Scissors: You'll need a good, sharp pair of fabric scissors to cut out the flower petals.

Tube/point turner: You will need a small tube/point turner for turning the flower petals and leaves right side out. You can find these in the notions section of your local fabric store.

Resealable plastic bags: Resealable plastic bags are a great way to keep organized. I store extra bits of embellishing threads, beads, and fabric scraps in them. They come in several sizes and are available at most craft stores, or look for snack-size bags at the grocery store. I use them to store all my extra leaves, stems, and flowers.

basic quilt CONSTRUCTION

The projects in this book require that you quilt—and often bind—the quilt top before appliquéing the dimensional flowers. The following pages provide the information you will need to construct the backdrop for your floral appliqués.

selecting the background fabric

Choosing the proper fabric for the background of your quilt is an important decision. When looking at a quilt, the background should be just that—in the background. The color should complement the overall design, not overwhelm it.

I like the background fabric to suggest that something is going on just out of view or that the sun is shining behind the design. A solid or solid-looking fabric is the most effective.

Contrast is very important between the background fabric and the other elements of the design. I lay the fabrics I have chosen for the other elements of the quilt on top of the background fabric and view everything from about six feet away. If the contrast is good and the colors seem to work together, I begin working on the project.

Once you have chosen the fabric for the background, cut two pieces: one for the front of the quilt and one for the back of the quilt. I like my background and backing fabrics to be the same because it makes choosing a quilting thread color easy and it means I don't have to worry about bobbin threads showing on the front of the quilt. Cut the backing and batting 1" or so larger than the desired finished size of the quilt, because the layers will draw up (shrink) as you quilt. The extra batting and fabric allow you to square up the quilt after the quilting is done.

basting the layers

Basting the layers of a quilt properly is one of the most important steps for ensuring a smooth, flat quilt. Lay the backing fabric wrong side up on a clean, flat surface and smooth out any wrinkles. Place the batting on top of the backing, making sure the edges are even. Ease out any lumps or bumps in the batting. Center the quilt top right side up on the batting; smooth out any

wrinkles in all the layers, making sure everything is flat and even.

I prefer to pin baste using #1 brass safety pins. You can find these pins at any quilt store. Start pinning in the middle of the quilt and work your way to the edges, placing the pins about a fist's width apart. Smooth out the layers as you go. Be sure to pin the corners and edges of the quilt. Temporary spray adhesive is another option for keeping the layers together. Spray the wrong side of the fabrics, not the batting, when using this product. Turn the quilt over and make sure the backing and batting are smooth and flat.

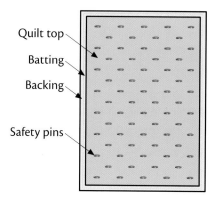

Quilt top
Batting
Backing
Safety pins

choosing a quilting design

After the layers of your quilt are basted together, you need to decide on the quilting design. I don't like to mark quilting patterns on my quilt. I choose simple designs that I stitch without marking. Stippling, swirls, and loops are the easiest to master. Try echo quilting the stems or leaves. If you want, you could machine appliqué the stems and echo quilt them at the same time. This adds a little dimension to the stems, making them pop off the surface. The scope of quilting designs is limited only by your imagination, so doodle on paper until you find a design that will work for your quilt. If you need more design ideas and inspiration, look for one of the dozens of books available on the subject of machine quilting.

Stippling

Swirls

Loop-de-loop   Loops and hearts

Swirls and triangles   Swirls and petals

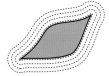

Echo quilting

quilting the layers

I like to machine quilt my quilts because it's fast and easy. I quilt my background fabric before I add the stems and flowers, because it is almost impossible to quilt around the dimensional flowers once they have been appliquéd to the background. If you prefer, you can appliqué the stems to the background before quilting and then echo quilt around them, or you can hand quilt the project, either before or after the flowers and stems have been appliquéd in place.

squaring up the quilt

After the quilting is done, square up the quilt. Starting at one corner of the quilt, straighten two adjacent sides by trimming them with a square ruler and rotary cutter. Move to the opposite corner and square the remaining two sides. Check the corners against each other to make sure the sides are straight and true. Adjust them as needed. On small-scale quilts, even slight misalignments will show, so take your time and make sure your quilt is straight and square.

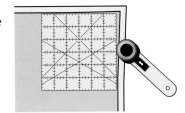

adding accent trim

A great way to boost the visual interest of a quilt is by adding a contrasting fabric accent before sewing on the binding. See "Two-Tone Folded-Petal Flowers" (page 43) for an example.

1. Measure the width of the quilt top. From the accent fabric, cut two 1"-wide strips the length measured plus 5". With wrong sides together, fold the strip in half to measure ½" wide; press the length of the strip.

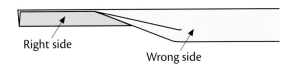

Right side

Wrong side

2. With the raw edges aligned, center and glue-baste the accent strips to the top and bottom edges of the quilt. Trim the ends of the accent strips even with the quilt sides.

Raw edges

Raw edges

3. Repeat steps 1 and 2 to measure the length of the quilt top, cut the accent strips, and glue-baste them in place. Trim the ends of the accent strips even with the top and bottom edges of the quilt.

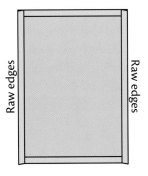

Raw edges

Raw edges

4. Stitch the binding to the quilt, following the instructions in the next section.

binding the quilt

The binding on a quilt is like a frame, and the choice of binding fabric can really make a big difference in the overall impression. Choose a fabric that somehow relates to the body of the quilt in color or design. I like to repeat one of the fabrics in the quilt for the binding. Because all the quilts in this book are small, one double-fold, straight-of-grain fabric strip is sufficient for the binding.

1. Cut a 2½"-wide strip across the fabric width (from selvage to selvage). With wrong sides together, fold the strip in half lengthwise to measure 1¼" wide; press the length of the strip.

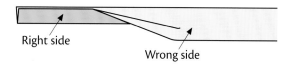

Right side

Wrong side

2. Align the binding raw edge with the quilt raw edge. Leave 5" or 6" of the binding free and start sewing in the middle of one side of the quilt, using a ³⁄₈"-wide seam allowance. Stop sewing ³⁄₈" from the corner of the quilt.

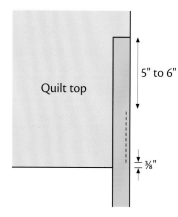

Quilt top

5" to 6"

³⁄₈"

3. Turn the quilt counterclockwise 90°. Fold the binding up so that the fold forms a 45° angle. Fold the binding back down on itself, aligning the raw edges of the binding and the quilt. Start stitching on the edge of the quilt. Repeat with the remaining corners.

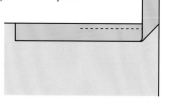

Start stitching.

4. Stop stitching about 5" from where the ends of the binding will be joined. Remove the quilt from the machine. Fold one end of the binding back on itself about 2". Fold the other end of the binding back on itself so that the folded ends butt together; crease the folds.

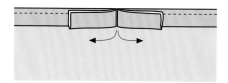

Butt the folds together.

5. Unfold the binding. With right sides together, line up the creases and sew directly on the creased line. Test the strip to make sure it fits without any excess fabric. Trim the excess binding ¼" from the seam and press the seam open.

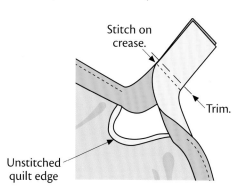

Stitch on crease.

Trim.

Unstitched quilt edge

6. Refold the binding and finish sewing it to the quilt. Fold the binding over the raw edge of the quilt and hand stitch it to the back of the quilt with a blind stitch. The folded binding will form a miter at each corner. Secure the corners on the front of the quilt with a few blind stitches.

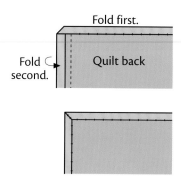

Fold first.

Fold second.

Quilt back

FLOWER construction

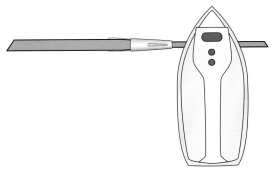

Before creating flowers in fabric, it's a good idea to have a basic understanding of flower anatomy.

diagram of a flower

Without getting too technical, here are some basic terms I refer to in the book that may or may not be familiar to you.

Petal: The leaflike part of the flower, often brightly colored to attract insects

Stamen: The pollen-bearing part of the flower

Calyx: The collective name for the outermost ring of joined floral parts protecting the bud; usually green, but can be brightly colored as well

Stem: The part of the plant that supports the leaves and flowers

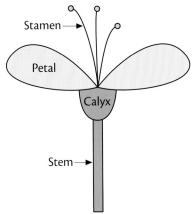

diagram of a leaf

Leaves are usually green and grow from the stem of the plant. Although leaf shapes can be very complex, the basic construction of all leaves is the same.

Stem: The part of the leaf that connects it to the plant

Center vein: The main artery of the leaf, which runs from the stem to the leaf tip

Side veins: The smaller veins that branch off the main artery

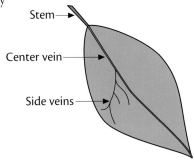

making stems and vines

Bias strips are used to shape the flower stems and vines. I prefer to use a bias-tape maker to make my strips. Starting with a ¼-yard cut of fabric will allow you to cut strips as long as 12".

MAKING BIAS TAPE

1. Position a ruler on the fabric with the 45°-angle mark lined up along the selvage edge. (The side of the ruler will be on the bias of the fabric.) Using a rotary cutter, cut along the edge of the ruler. Measuring from the cut edge, cut strips the width indicated for the project. Cut as many strips as you need to total the required length for the project you are making.

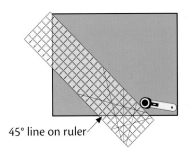

45° line on ruler

2. Spray the strips of fabric with starch. Allow the fabric to absorb the starch or the starch will flake when ironed. Insert one end of the strip of fabric into the wide end of the tape maker and pull it out the narrow end to fold under the long edges. Pull the tape maker along the length of the strip, pressing the folded strip with a steam iron. Allow the fabric to cool before you remove it from the pressing surface.

3. Cut the tape to the length needed for stems and vines.

Leaves enhance a floral design by adding balance and fullness. Even a single flower needs the support of the stem and leaves.

BASIC LEAVES

When making these leaves, keep the form simple. Complex shapes are difficult to turn right side out smoothly. The example given here uses 4" x 22" strips to construct the basic leaves. Some of the projects call for slightly wider or narrower strips, and the leaves will vary in size accordingly, but the construction is the same.

1. Cut two 4" x 22" strips of green fabric and layer them right sides together. Fold the strips in half lengthwise to measure 2" x 22". Press the fold to mark the center of the strips. Unfold the strips of fabric, but keep them layered.

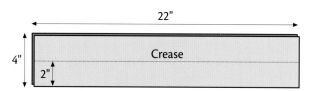

2. Set your machine to sew between 15 and 20 stitches per inch—about 1.5 or less on some machines—and use matching green thread.

3. Starting at one end of the layered strips, insert the needle into the fabric at the bottom edge and sew one side of a simple leaf shape. Stop with the needle in the down position when you reach the center crease. Lift the presser foot, pivot the fabric, and sew the other side of the leaf, stopping at the bottom of the fabric strip.

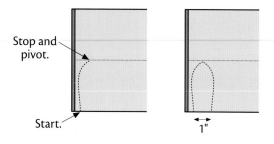

4. Lift the presser foot. Beginning about ½" from the first leaf, sew the next leaf. Continue making leaves ½" apart across the length of the strip until you reach the end, and then turn the fabric to begin sewing leaves along the other side of the strip. Alternate the leaf shapes so they interlock like zipper teeth between the leaves on the other

side of the strip, leaving ½" of space between the tops of the leaves. Don't cut the threads between the leaves and don't worry about variations in leaf shapes; it's what makes them look natural.

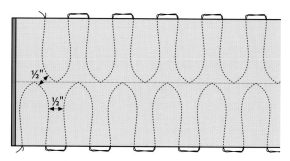

5. Using fabric scissors, cut out the leaves, adding a scant ¼" seam allowance. Don't cut too close to the stitching or you'll push through a seam when you turn the leaves right side out.

6. Use a point turner to turn the leaves right side out, and finger-press them into shape. Store the leaves in a plastic bag until you are ready to use them.

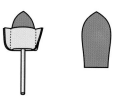

7. When you are ready to use the leaves, thread a hand-sewing needle with a double strand of matching thread. If the bottom raw edge of the leaf will be covered by a stem or flower, you can leave it raw; if not, turn up a scant ¼" hem on the bottom of the leaf and finger-press it in place. Stitch the opening closed, using a running stitch, and pull the thread to gather the bottom edge.

STUFFED LEAVES

These leaves are constructed in the same manner as basic leaves but with an added layer of batting to fill them out. As with basic leaves, it is important to keep the shape of these leaves simple or they will be difficult to turn to the right side.

1. Cut two 4" x 22" strips of green fabric (or the size specified in your project) and layer them right sides together. Fold the strips in half to measure 2" x 22". Press the fold to mark the center of the strips. Unfold the strips of fabric, but keep them layered. Center a 3½" x 22" strip of thin batting on top of the fabric strips, leaving ¼" of fabric exposed at the top and bottom edges. Turn the strip over so the batting is on the bottom.

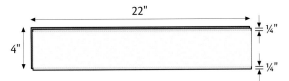

2. Follow steps 2–5 of "Basic Leaves" on page 10 to stitch the leaf shapes and cut them out. Trim the batting of each leaf up to the stitching line to reduce bulk.

3. Use a point turner inserted between the fabric layers to turn the leaves right side out and finger-press into shape. Turn up a scant ¼" hem around the bottom of the leaf, making sure the fabric covers the batting, and finger-press it in place.

4. With your machine still set at 15 to 20 stitches per inch and using matching thread, stitch the center vein and all the side veins of the leaf. Go around the edge of the leaf to jump to the side veins. Stitch around the outside edges of the leaf, stitching across the previous "jump" stitches. Backstitch several times to lock your stitching.

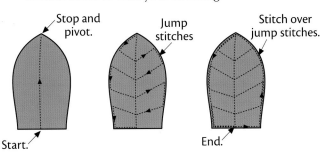

Stop and pivot.   Jump stitches   Stitch over jump stitches.

Start.   End.

FUSED LEAVES

Fused leaves are two-sided and flexible. They are very easy to make and their shape can be simple or complex.

Sample leaf shapes

1. Cut two pieces of fabric about 1" larger than the leaf design you are going to make. Insert a piece of regular-weight, sewable, fusible web between the two fabric pieces and fuse them together, following the manufacturer's instructions. Allow the fabric to cool.

2. Draw the leaf shape onto the fused fabric piece using your favorite marking method.

3. Set your sewing machine to sew between 15 and 20 stitches per inch and use matching or contrasting thread. Stitch the center vein and all the side veins of the leaf. Go around the edge of the leaf to jump to the side veins.

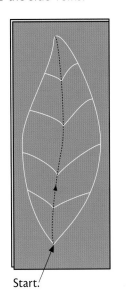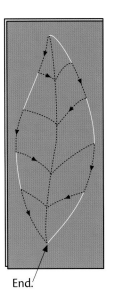

Start.   End.

4. Change the stitch on your machine to a narrow zigzag. Starting at the bottom of the leaf (where the stem will be), stitch around the leaf's outside edge, pivoting at any points. Stop, pivot, and stitch up the stem, and then turn the leaf to stitch over the stem a second time for added thickness. Backstitch several times to lock your stitching.

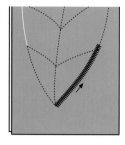

5. Using fabric scissors, cut out the leaf close to, but not through, the outside stitching. Press the leaf with steam to set the stitches.

6. Tack the leaf in place. Because it is finished on both sides, you only need to tack it down in a few places. If you like, put a few tucks in the leaf for a more realistic look.

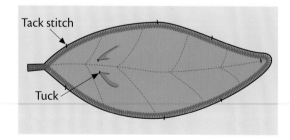

Tack stitch

Tuck

making a calyx

The calyx is made in the same manner as basic leaves except that the shape is rounded at the top rather than pointed. The hump-shaped piece is used for several of the flowers and flower buds in this book.

1. Refer to "Basic Leaves" on page 10 for cutting, layering, folding, and sewing instructions, but follow the diagram below for shape and spacing.

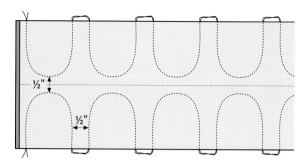

½"

½"

2. Using fabric scissors, cut out the calyxes, adding a scant ¼" seam allowance. Don't cut too close to the stitching or you'll push through a seam when you turn the shapes right side out. Use a point turner to turn the calyxes right side out, and finger-press them into shape. Turn up a scant ⅛" hem around the bottom of each calyx; finger-press it in place.

⅛" hem

3. Insert the raw edges of a flower or flower bud into the prepared calyx. Make sure all the raw edges of the flower are covered by the calyx. Using a hand-sewing needle with thread to match the calyx, blindstitch the calyx to the flower along the hemmed edge, pulling the thread to slightly gather.

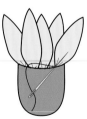

making basic prairie point flowers

You can use this simple folding technique to construct stunning flowers. The example given here uses five 2" squares for each flower. This is a common size; however, some projects call for more or fewer petals and slightly smaller or larger squares of fabric. Follow the same basic instructions to make the prairie points, and then assemble them following the instructions given for the specific flower you are making.

1. Cut five 2" squares of fabric. Fold each square of fabric in half diagonally, wrong sides together, and finger-press the fold. Fold the triangles in half again and finger-press the folds to complete the prairie points.

2. Thread a hand-sewing needle with a double strand of thread that matches the fabric; knot the ends together. Holding a prairie point in your hand with the open folds to your left and the raw edges at the top, stitch about ¼" from the raw edges. When you reach the end of the piece, begin sewing onto the next prairie point and stitch across it. Keep adding prairie points in this manner until all five are stitched together with a continuous line of stitching.

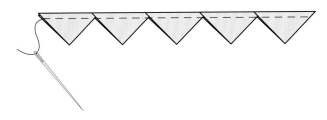

3. Loop around and join the last prairie point to the first prairie point, pulling the thread snug while pushing the raw edges of the petals to the back of the flower. Stitch through the raw edges on the back of the flower petals several times to lock the shape, and then knot the thread.

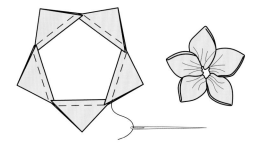

4. Embellish the flower center with threads or beads, or cover it with a yo-yo (see page 14).

making double-folded prairie point flowers

The double-folded prairie point flower is created by folding a square of fabric a little differently than the regular prairie point flower. An extra fold gives the flowers a more dramatic look. The example given here uses five 2" squares of fabric to construct the flower; however, some projects call for more or fewer petals, and slightly smaller or larger squares. Use the same basic technique to make the double-folded prairie points, and then assemble them following the instructions given for the specific flower you are making.

1. Cut five 2" squares of fabric. Fold each square in half horizontally, wrong sides together, and finger-press the fold. Fold the upper-right corners to the bottom centers and finger-press the folds. Fold the upper-left corners to the bottom centers and finger-press the folds.

2. Thread a hand-sewing needle with a double strand of matching thread; knot the ends together. Holding a double-folded prairie point in your hand with the open folds facing up and the raw edges at the top, stitch about ¼" from the raw edges. When you reach the end of the piece, begin sewing into the next double-folded prairie point and stitch across it. Add prairie points in this manner until all five are joined with a continuous line of stitching. Make sure the open folds are all facing up before you add each one.

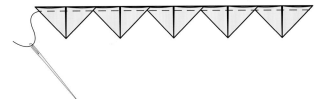

3. Loop the last prairie point around and join it to the first one, pulling the thread snug while pushing the raw edges of the petals to the back of the flower. Stitch through the raw edges on the back of the flower petals several times to lock the shape, and then knot the thread.

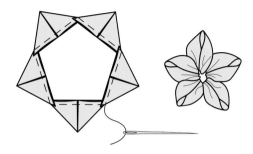

4. Embellish the flower center with threads or beads, or cover it with a yo-yo (see below right).

making ruched flowers

You can form a wide range of flowers by stitching various patterns into a strip of fabric that has been folded in half lengthwise, wrong sides together. Always begin stitching at the raw edges of the fabric strip, stitch toward the fold, and then back toward the raw edges, using a double strand of thread. After you are done stitching, pull the ends of the thread to gather, or ruche, the strip. Each pattern has changes in the shape and proportion; the shape of the pattern affects the shape of the petal. You can stitch these patterns into a single petal or bud, and you can change the look of the finished petal or flower depending on how tightly or loosely you pull the thread.

Following are some stitching ideas for ruched flowers. The projects in the book will indicate what pattern to stitch, but the possibilities are endless. Try creating your own designs to make other fabulous flowers.

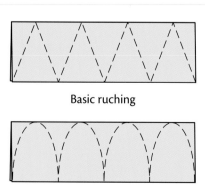

Basic ruching

Shell ruching

Trapezoid ruching

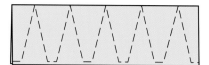

Heart monitor ruching

Half oval ruching

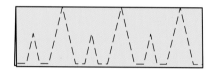

Irregular heartbeat ruching

making strip-pieced flowers

Just as the name suggests, these flowers start with a strip set made from two strips of fabric. One strip is always green because it will become the calyx; the other strip will become the flower. The strip set is crosscut into smaller segments and each segment is shaped into a flower. Each project will give specific instructions for making the flowers.

To make a strip set, align one long edge of a flower strip and a calyx strip, right sides together; stitch using a ¼" seam allowance. Press the seam allowance toward the flower fabric. Crosscut the strip set into segments as indicated in the project instructions.

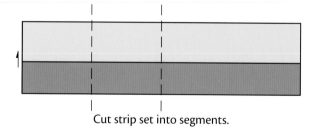

Cut strip set into segments.

making yo-yos

The simple and versatile yo-yo can be used to make flowers or to finish a flower center. I love making yo-yos because they are so quick and easy!

CUTTING FABRIC CIRCLES

A yo-yo is made by gathering the edge of a fabric circle. The projects in this book provide patterns for making circle templates, but you can also use the following template-free method if you wish.

To quickly and easily cut circles from fabric without using a template, cut squares of fabric in the desired diameter of the finished circle, such as 2". Use fabric scissors to trim the squares into circles. Don't worry about making perfect circles; once the fabric is gathered, the circles will look perfect.

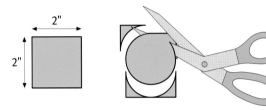

BASIC YO-YOS

Using a running stitch, hand stitch a scant ¼" hem around your prepared circle. Stitch closer to the raw edge of the circle than to the folded edge. Pull the thread tightly to gather the center of the circle with the right side of the fabric facing out. Use your finger to flatten and distribute the gathers around the circle. Stitch through a few gathers to lock the shape. Push the thread to the wrong side of the circle and make a knot. Sew the yo-yo to the quilt with the gathered side up.

RAW-EDGED YO-YOS

On the right side of the yo-yo fabric, hand sew a running stitch around the outside edge of the circle, about ¼" from the raw edge. Pull the thread tightly to gather the center of the circle. Use your fingers to flatten and distribute the gathers. Tie off the thread, hiding the knot inside the circle. Sew the yo-yo to the quilt with the gathered side down.

beading

Some of the quilts include beading as an embellishment, usually in the flower centers. In some cases the beads are adhered in place with embellishing glue. In other instances, the beads are added individually using a stab stitch (going down through the fabric and then back up again in two separate motions), or are strung and couched to the quilt by hand as described in "Couching Threads for Embellishment" below. The individual project instructions will tell you the number, color, and type of beads to use, and suggest which method to use for attaching them.

couching threads for embellishment

Couching is a method of attaching almost any thread, including heavy or highly textured threads or yarns, to the surface of fabric by using a finer thread to work small stitches over the embellishing thread. You can couch by hand or machine and you can use either contrasting or matching thread over the top, depending on the look you want.

To hand stitch, use a simple tack stitch over the top of the embellishing thread.

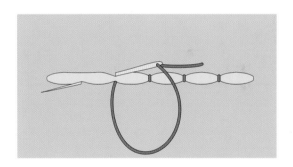

To machine stitch, use a straight stitch or a zigzag stitch to secure the embellishing thread into place.

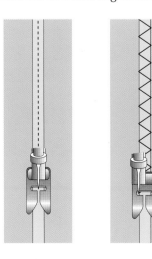

These flowers are truly stars! Simple folding techniques, a few beads, and some embellishing threads make them fast, fun, and easy. Change the colors of the petals or the embellishing threads to suit your fancy, or let your imagination run wild and sew up a garden full of unexpected delights.

FIVE-PETAL
starflowers

materials

2 pieces, 8" x 9", of tone-on-tone white fabric for background and backing

1 strip, 2½" x 42", of lime green fabric for binding

2 strips, 3" x 22", of light green fabric for leaves

2 strips, 2" x 28", of lime green fabric for large flowers

1 strip, 1¼" x 27", of lime green fabric for small flowers

8" x 9" piece of thin, dense batting

Sewing thread to match fabrics

2 yards of lime green multi-ply chenille cord or textured yarn for stems and flower centers (You need a minimum of 7 plies.)

1 yard of green eyelash yarn for grass

45 small green bugle beads

making the quilt top

Unlike a standard appliqué quilt, this project requires that you quilt and bind the quilt before adding the appliquéd flowers. Work through the following steps, referring to "Basic Quilt Construction" (page 6) as needed.

1. Layer the backing, batting, and background pieces.

2. Baste and quilt the layers, and then square the quilt to 6¼" x 7¾".

3. Use the lime green 2½" x 42" strip to make the binding and finish the edges of the quilt.

making the flowers

1. Crosscut the two lime green 2" x 28" strips into 25 squares, 2" x 2".

2. Thread a hand-sewing needle with thread to match the lime green fabric. Referring to "Making Basic Prairie Point Flowers" (page 12), fold the squares into prairie points. Join five petals, pulling the thread to gather the petals slightly. Stitch through the petals several times to lock the flower shape; knot the thread on the back of the flower. Make five large flowers.

Make 5.

3. Crosscut the lime green 1¼" x 27" strip into 20 squares, 1¼" x 1¼". Repeat step 2 to make four small flowers.

4. Cut the chenille cord or textured yarn into two 1-yard lengths, one for the flower stems and one for the flower centers. Separate one of the lengths into single-ply pieces. Wrap one ply around two fingers 8 to 10 times, and then twist the loop into a figure-eight shape. Place the twisted loop of yarn on the center of a large flower and, using a needle threaded with thread to match the flower, stab stitch through the center of the loop. With the thread still attached, use a stab stitch to sew five beads in the center of the flower; knot the thread on the back of the flower. Repeat for all five large flowers.

5. Cut two of the remaining single-ply cord pieces into half-yard lengths. Wrap a length around one finger 8 to 10 times, and then twist the loops into a figure-eight shape. Place the twisted loop of yarn on the center of a small flower and stab stitch through the center of the loop. Use a stab stitch

to sew five beads in the center of the flower; knot the thread on the back of the flower. Repeat for all four small flowers.

making the leaves

Referring to "Basic Leaves" (page 10), use the two light green 3" x 22" strips to make 14 leaves. Each leaf should measure ½" wide at the bottom and vary from 1¼" to 2¾" high. Cut out the leaves and turn them right side out, finger-pressing them into shape. Turn up a ⅛" hem around the bottom of each leaf and finger-press it in place. Use matching green thread to tightly gather the bottom of each leaf.

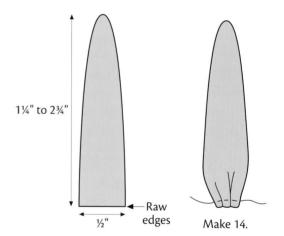

1¼" to 2¾"

½" — Raw edges

Make 14.

finishing

Refer to the quilt photo on page 16 as needed.

1. Cut the 1-yard length of cord that has not been separated into six 6"-long pieces for the stems. Referring to "Couching Threads for Embellishment" (page 15), couch the cord to the background for the flower stems.

2. Appliqué the large flowers and one small flower to the tops of the stems. Appliqué the remaining three flowers to the background fabric. Tack the leaves to the stems, twisting and turning them as desired.

3. Twist the green eyelash yarn together and couch it to the bottom of the quilt to form the grass, leaving the ends to dangle for added texture.

The yo-yo center and single sparkly bead make this perky five-petal flower irresistible. Play with different color combinations to create an endless array of sweet little flowers.

mini FIVE-PETAL
flowers

materials

2 pieces, 7" x 7", of blue fabric for background and backing

1 strip, 2½" x 42", of yellow fabric for binding

3 strips, 1¼" x 42", of yellow fabric for flowers petals

1 strip, 1½" x 20", of orange fabric for flower centers

¼ yard of green fabric for stems and leaves

7" x 7" piece of thin, dense batting

Sewing thread to match fabrics

⅓ yard of multicolored eyelash yarn

12 yellow seed beads, size 6/0

Template material

Water-soluble fabric glue

¼" bias-tape maker

making the quilt top

Unlike a standard appliqué quilt, this project requires that you quilt and bind the quilt before adding the appliquéd flowers. Work through the following steps, referring to "Basic Quilt Construction" (page 6) as needed.

1. Layer the backing, batting, and background pieces.

2. Baste and quilt the layers, and then square the quilt to 6" x 6".

3. Use the yellow 2½" x 42" strip to make the binding and finish the edges of the quilt.

Finished size: 6" x 6"

making the flowers

1. Crosscut the three yellow 1¼" x 42" strips into 60 squares, 1¼" x 1¼".

2. Thread a hand-sewing needle with thread to match the yellow fabric. Referring to "Making Basic Prairie Point Flowers" (page 12), fold the squares into prairie points. Join five petals, pulling the thread to gather the petals slightly. Stitch through the petals several times to lock the flower shape; knot the thread on the back of the flower. Make 12 flowers.

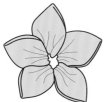

Make 12.

3. Use the pattern below right to make a flower center template from the template material. Use the template to cut 12 circles from the orange 1 ½" x 20" strip. Refer to "Basic Yo-Yos" (page 15) to gather each circle into a tightly gathered yo-yo.

4. Thread a hand-sewing needle with thread to match the orange fabric. Blindstitch one yo-yo to the center of a flower, making sure all the raw edges of the flower are covered by the yo-yo. Knot the thread on the back of the flower but do not cut it. Push the needle up through the center of the yo-yo and thread one seed bead onto the needle. Go back down through the yo-yo to the back of the flower and knot the thread. Repeat for all 12 flowers.

making the stems and leaves

1. Referring to "Making Stems and Vines" (page 9), make six 12"-long pieces of ¼"-wide bias tape from the green fabric. Fold the strips in half to measure ⅛" wide; press. Refer to the quilt photo at left to cut the stems into varying lengths.

⅛"

2. Referring to "Basic Leaves" (page 10), use the remaining green fabric to cut two 3" x 10" strips and make 12 leaves. Each leaf should measure about ⅜" wide at the bottom and 1" high. Cut out the leaves and turn them right side out, finger-pressing them into shape. Turn up a ⅛" hem around the bottom of each leaf and finger-press it in place. Use matching green thread to tightly gather the bottom of each leaf.

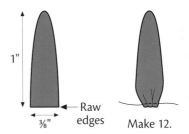

1"

⅜"   Raw edges

Make 12.

finishing

Refer to the quilt photo at left as needed.

1. Glue-baste the stems to the prepared background fabric. Appliqué them in place. Appliqué the flowers to the tops of the stems. Appliqué the leaves to the stems.

2. Referring to "Couching Threads for Embellishment" (page 15), couch the multicolored eyelash yarn to the bottom of the stems to form the grass, leaving the ends to dangle for added texture.

Flower center
Cut 12.

Finished size: 7" x 10"

Celebrate summer with sunflowers! A visual delight for young and old,

sunflowers are native to North America, where they are wildly popular in the garden.

Warm and inviting, these sunflowers are as easy to make as they are to recognize.

SUNFLOWERS

materials

2 pieces, 8" x 11", of light blue fabric for background and backing

1 strip, 2½" x 42", of mottled yellowish orange fabric for binding

3 strips, 1½" x 42", of mottled yellowish orange fabric for flowers

1 piece, 2" x 12", of brown fabric for flower centers

1 piece, 6" x 9", of basket-weave print for basket

2 pieces, 6" x 11", of green fabric for leaves

1 piece, 1½" x 9", of scrap batting for flower centers

8" x 11" piece of thin, dense batting

Sewing thread to match fabrics

300 black seed beads, size 6/0

6" x 11" piece of sewable fusible web

Water-soluble fabric glue

Template material

making the quilt top

Unlike a standard appliqué quilt, this project requires that you quilt and bind the quilt before adding the appliquéd flowers. Work through the following steps, referring to "Basic Quilt Construction" (page 6) as needed.

1. Layer the backing, 8" x 11" batting, and background pieces.

2. Baste and quilt the layers, and then square the quilt to 7" x 10".

3. Use the mottled yellowish orange 2½" x 42" strip to make the binding and finish the edges of the quilt.

making the basket

1. From the basket-weave piece, cut two 1" x 9" strips for the basket handles. Fold each strip in half lengthwise, wrong sides together. Sew ¼" from the long edges of each strip. Turn the strips right side out. With the seam along one edge, press each strip.

2. Trace the basket pattern on page 25 onto the wrong side of the remaining basket fabric, and cut it out. Press under a ¼" seam allowance around all the edges of the basket.

3. Referring to the photo on page 22, position the basket on the prepared background, making sure the basket bottom edge is square with the bottom edge of your quilt. Insert one end of each basket handle behind the sides of the basket. Place the other end of each handle at the center of the basket top edge. Adjust the handles until they are even and centered; trim any excess fabric behind the basket to reduce bulk. Glue-baste the handles to the basket. Glue-baste the basket to the background fabric and appliqué it in place.

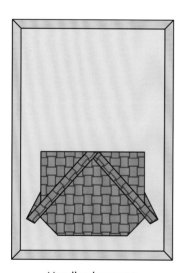

Handle placement

making the leaves

1. Use the patterns on page 25 to make small, medium, and large leaf templates from the template material.

2. Referring to "Fused Leaves" (page 11), use the templates, the 6" x 11" pieces of green fabric, and the fusible web to make five large leaves, three medium leaves, and three small leaves. Use matching green thread to topstitch the center and side veins on each leaf, following the patterns. Zigzag stitch around the outer edge of each leaf. Cut out the leaves and then press each one to set the topstitching.

making the flowers

1. Crosscut the mottled yellowish orange 1½" x 42" strips into 84 squares, 1½" x 1½".

2. Thread a hand-sewing needle with thread to match the yellowish orange fabric. Referring to "Making Basic Prairie Point Flowers" (page 12), fold the squares into prairie points. Join 12 to 15 petals, pulling the thread slightly to gather the petals into a ring. There will be a large gap in the center. Use your fingers to evenly distribute the gathers; knot the thread. Make six flowers.

Make 6.

3. Use the patterns on page 25 to make sunflower center templates for the fabric and batting. Use the fabric template to cut six circles from the brown 2" x 12" strip and the batting template to cut six circles from the 1½" x 9" batting scrap.

4. Referring to "Raw-Edged Yo-Yos" (page 15), make a raw-edged yo-yo from one of the brown circles. Gather the yo-yo slightly; do not cut or knot the thread. Insert a batting circle into the yo-yo. Pull the thread to gather the yo-yo around the batting; knot the thread. With the raw edges down, blind-stitch a yo-yo to the center of a flower, making sure all the raw edges of the flower are covered by the yo-yo. Knot the thread on the back of the flower.

Batting

5. Repeat step 4 to make stuffed yo-yos from the remaining brown circles and stitch them to the center of each flower.

6. Stitch a ring of approximately 50 black seed beads around each flower center. You can add the beads individually or string them and then couch them in place. Refer to "Beading" (page 15) and "Couching Threads for Embellishment" (page 15) for instructions for the desired method. Pull the thread to nestle the beads into the gap between the flower center and the petals; knot the thread but do not cut it. Finish by stab stitching one bead in the center of the flower, pulling the thread to nestle the bead into the batting. Knot the thread on the back of the flower.

finishing

Refer to the quilt photo on page 22 as needed.

1. Tack the leaves to the background.

2. Appliqué the flowers to the basket and background.

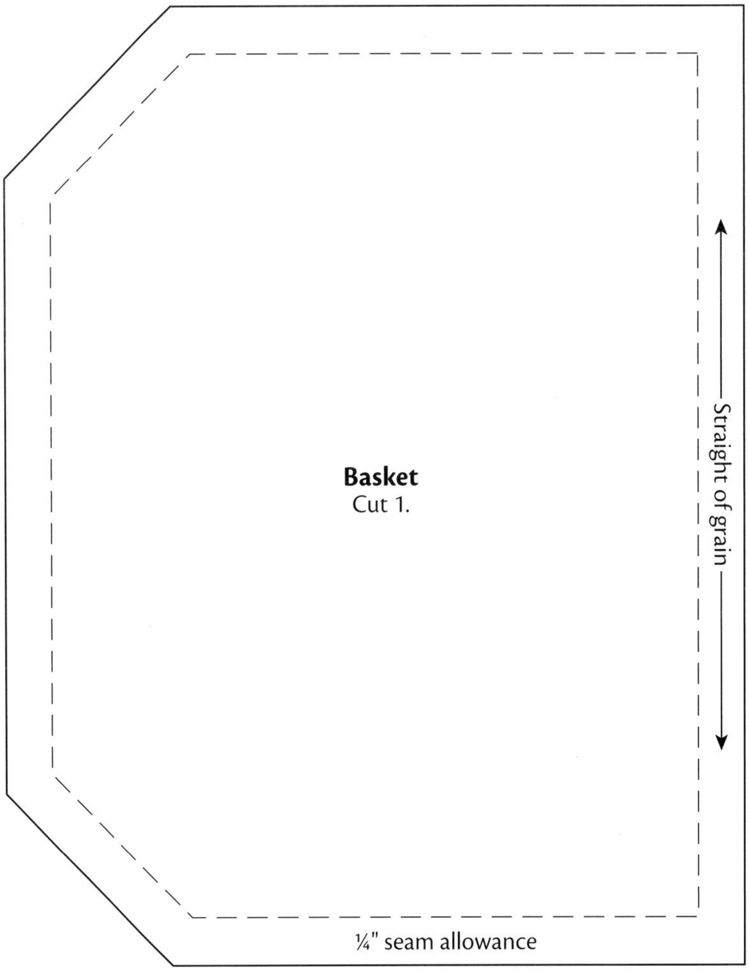

Basket
Cut 1.

Straight of grain

¼" seam allowance

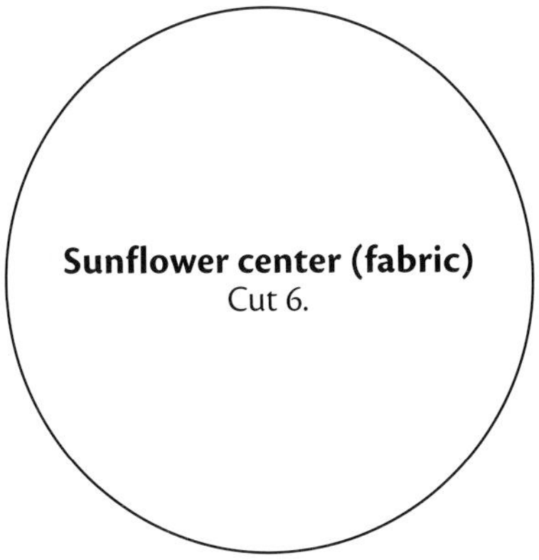

Sunflower center (fabric)
Cut 6.

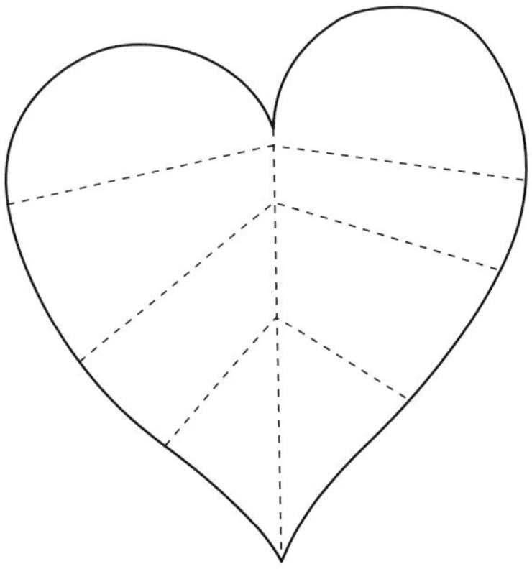

Large sunflower leaf
Make 5.

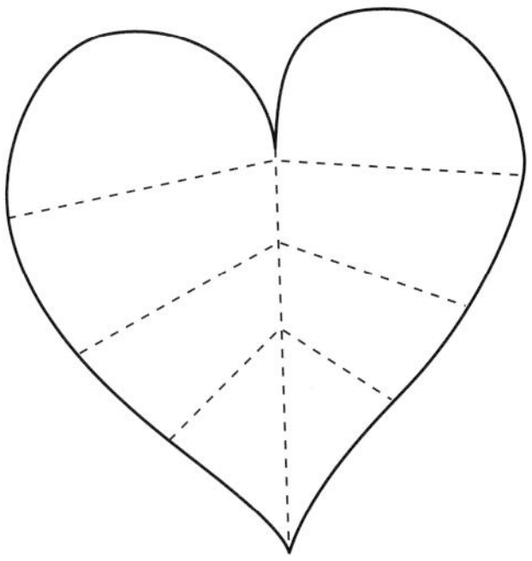

Medium sunflower leaf
Make 3.

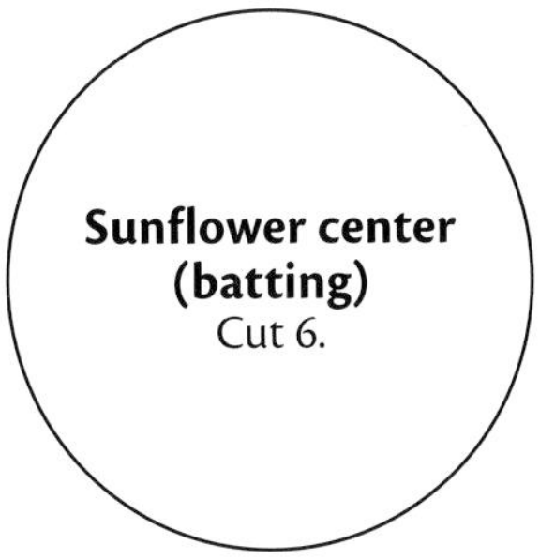

Sunflower center (batting)
Cut 6.

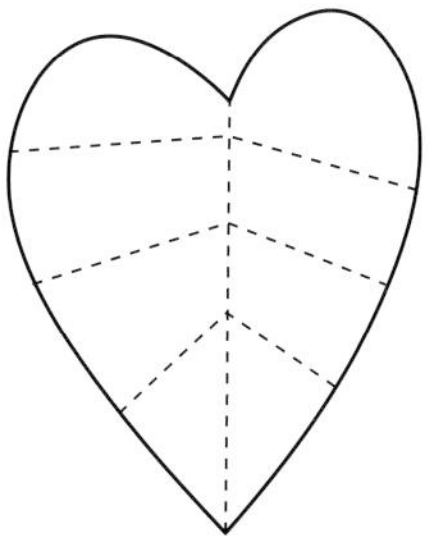

Small sunflower leaf

I love two-color daffodils! These are made with yellow petals and orange cups, but you could reverse the color placement if you'd like. Look through flower catalogs for other color combinations . . . the possibilities are endless!

DAFFODILS

materials

2 pieces, 9½" x 11½", of blue fabric for background and backing

2 strips, 2¼" x 42", of yellow fabric for flower petals

1 strip, 2" x 20", of orange fabric for flower center cups

¼ yard of green fabric for stems, leaves, and calyxes

1 strip, 2½" x 42", of yellow fabric for binding

9½" x 11½" piece of thin, dense batting

Sewing thread to match fabrics

½ yard of green embellishing yarn for grass

5 yellow drop beads, size 4.5 mm, for flower centers

Assorted yellow and orange seed beads, size 10/0, for grass accents

Water-soluble fabric glue

¼" bias-tape maker

making the quilt top

Unlike a standard appliqué quilt, this project requires that you quilt the quilt before adding the appliquéd flowers. Work through the following steps, referring to "Basic Quilt Construction" (page 6) as needed.

1. Layer the backing, batting, and background pieces.

2. Baste and quilt the layers, and then square the quilt to 8½" x 10½". Don't bind the quilt yet.

making the flowers

1. Crosscut the yellow 2¼" x 42" strips into 33 squares, 2¼" x 2¼".

2. Thread a hand-sewing needle with thread to match the yellow fabric. Referring to "Making Basic Prairie Point Flowers" (page 12), fold the squares into prairie points. Join six petals, pulling the thread to gather the petals slightly. Stitch through the petals several times to lock the flower shape; knot the thread on the back of the flower. Make five flowers. You will have three petals left for the two flower buds.

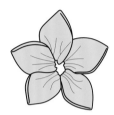

Make 5.

3. Press under a ¼"-wide hem along both long sides of the orange 2" x 20" strip. Fold the strip in half lengthwise, wrong sides together; press. The strip should now measure ¾" x 20".

4. Crosscut the strip into five segments, 3¼" wide. Press under a ¼" hem on one end of each section. With right sides out, loop the raw edge of each strip around and into the finished edge of the strip. Use matching thread to blindstitch the seam.

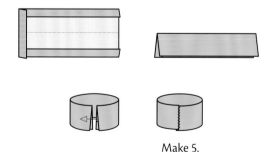

Make 5.

5. Use a running stitch to gather the bottom edge of each strip tightly to form a cup shape. Pass the needle through the bottom edge several times to lock the shape; knot the thread.

6. Use matching thread to blindstitch a cup to the center of each flower, making sure to cover all the raw edges of the flower. Stitch through the flower and cup several times to lock the shape; knot the thread but do not cut it. Push the needle up through the center of the flower and stab stitch a drop bead to the center of the flower, pulling the thread slightly to nestle the bead into the flower. Pass the needle back through the center of the flower to the back of the flower, and then knot and cut the thread. Make five flowers.

7. Cut the remainder of the orange strip into one 2" section and one 1¾" section. Refer to step 5 to stitch the two sections into small cups.

8. Stitch two of the remaining prairie points together, pulling the thread slightly to gather; do not cut the thread. Insert the 2" cup between the prairie points and stitch the petals to the cup, pulling the thread tightly to gather; knot the thread.

9. Wrap the remaining prairie point around the 1¾" cup. Stitch the petal and cup together along the bottom edges, and pull the thread tightly to gather.

making the leaves, stems, and calyxes

1. Referring to "Basic Leaves" (page 10), cut two 6" x 11" strips from the green fabric and make seven leaves as shown. (You will not need to crease the strip and will be stitching across its entire width.) Each leaf shape should measure about ½" wide at the bottom and 5" high. Cut out the leaves and turn them right side out, finger-pressing them into shape.

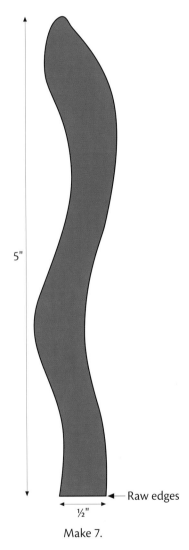

5"

←— Raw edges

½"

Make 7.

2. Referring to "Making Bias Tape" (page 9), use the remaining green fabric to make 40" of ¼"-wide bias tape. Refer to the quilt photo (page 26) to cut the strips into seven stems of varying lengths. Glue-baste the stems to the prepared background fabric, aligning one raw end of each stem with the bottom raw edge of the quilt. Appliqué the stems to the background fabric.

3. Glue-baste the bottom of the leaves to the bottom edge of the quilt, aligning the raw edges.

4. Referring to "Binding the Quilt" (page 8), use the yellow 2½" x 42" strip to make the binding and finish the edges of the quilt. Make sure the raw edges of the leaves and stems are covered by the binding.

5. Referring to "Making a Calyx" (page 12), use the remainder of the green fabric to make two ¾" x ¾" hump shapes to use as calyxes for the two flower buds. Cut out the calyxes and turn them right side out. Turn under a ⅛" hem around the bottom of each calyx; finger-press it in place. Insert a bud into each calyx, making sure all the raw edges of the bud are covered. Using matching green thread, blindstitch each calyx to a bud, pulling the thread slightly to gather.

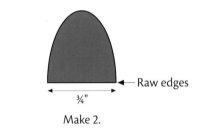

←— Raw edges

¾"

Make 2.

finishing

Refer to the quilt photo as needed.

1. Appliqué the five flowers and the two buds to the tops of the stems. Fold and twist the leaves as desired and tack them to the quilt.

2. Referring to "Couching Threads for Embellishment" (page 15), couch the green embellishing yarn along the bottom of the stems to form the grass. Stab stitch the yellow and orange seed beads along the grass for added color and texture.

Sometimes a single flower can make a big impact. This daffodil is very artistic with its wonderful orange shading. With very little time and effort you will be able to make a stunning gift for someone you love.

fancy DAFFODIL

materials

2 pieces, 6½" x 8", of blue fabric for background and backing

1 strip, 2½" x 16", of white fabric for flower petals

1 strip, 2" x 3¼", of white fabric for flower center cup

2 pieces, 4" x 10", of green fabric for leaves and stem

1 strip, 2½" x 42", of white fabric for binding

6½" x 8" piece of thin, dense batting

Sewing thread to match fabrics

¼ yard of iridescent green embellishing yarn for grass

¼ yard of decorative trim for accent in grass

1 yellow drop bead, size 4.5 mm, for flower center

15 orange seed beads, size 10/0, for grass accents

Orange oil pastel stick

Water-soluble fabric glue

Small stencil brush

¼" bias-tape maker

making the quilt top

Unlike a standard appliqué quilt, this project requires that you quilt the quilt top before adding the appliquéd flowers. Work through the following steps, referring to "Basic Quilt Construction" (page 6) as needed.

1. Layer the backing, batting, and background pieces.

2. Baste and quilt the layers, and then square the quilt to 5½" x 7". Don't bind the quilt yet.

making the flower

1. Crosscut the white 2½" x 16" strip into six squares, 2½" x 2½". Fold the squares in half diagonally, wrong sides together; finger-press the folds. Rub the stencil brush over the orange oil pastel stick and then brush the center of the fold of each square with the paint as shown.

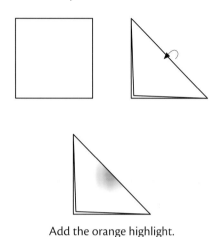

Add the orange highlight.

2. Referring to "Making Basic Prairie Point Flowers" (page 12), fold each triangle into a prairie point as shown, with the orange highlight on the outside of the fold; crease the folds. Thread a hand-sewing needle with white thread. Use a running stitch to join the six prairie points together, pulling the thread to gather the petals slightly. Stitch through the petals several times to lock the flower shape; knot the thread on the back of the flower.

Make 1.

3. Press under a ¼"-wide hem along both long sides of the white 2" x 3¼" strip. Press the strip in half lengthwise, wrong sides together. The strip should now measure ¾" x 3¼". Add the orange highlights to both sides of the fold, using the orange oil pastel stick and the stencil brush.

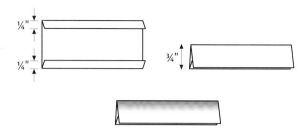

4. Press under a ¼"-wide hem on one end of the strip. With right sides out, loop the raw edge of the strip around and into the finished edge of the strip. Use white thread to blindstitch the seam.

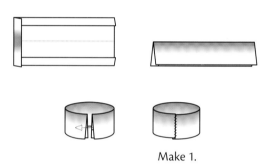

Make 1.

5. Use a running stitch to gather the bottom edge of the strip tightly to form a cup shape. Pass the needle through the bottom edge several times to lock the shape; knot the thread. Using the oil pastel stick and the stencil brush, add the highlight in the center of the flower cup.

6. Use white thread to blindstitch the cup to the center of the flower, making sure to cover all the raw edges of the flower. Stitch through the flower and cup several times to lock the shape; knot the thread but don't cut it yet. Push the needle up through the center of the flower and stab stitch the drop bead to the center of the flower, pulling the thread slightly to nestle the bead into the flower. Pass the needle back through the center of the flower to the back of the flower, and then knot and cut the thread.

making the leaves and stem

1. Referring to "Making Bias Tape" (page 9), use one of the green 4" x 10" pieces to make 5" of ¼"-wide bias tape for the stem. Glue-baste the stem to the background fabric, aligning one raw end of the stem with the bottom raw edge of the quilt. Appliqué the stem to the background fabric.

2. Referring to "Basic Leaves" (page 10), use the remainder of the green fabric piece from step 1 and the remaining green 4" x 10" piece to make two leaves as shown. (You will not need to crease the strip.) Start stitching at the short end of the pieces. Each leaf should measure ¾" wide at the bottom and 5" high. Cut out the leaves and turn them right side out, finger-pressing them into shape. Glue-baste the bottom of the leaves to the bottom edge of the quilt, aligning the raw edges.

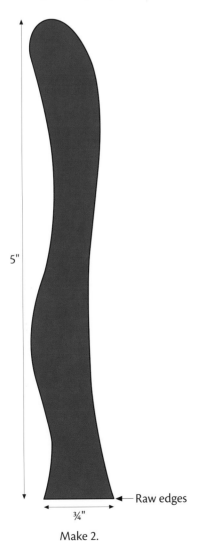

5"

¾"

← Raw edges

Make 2.

finishing

Refer to the quilt photo on page 30 as needed.

1. Referring to "Binding the Quilt" (page 8), use the white 2½" x 42" strip to make the binding. Use the oil pastel stick and the stencil brush to add the highlight to one side of the binding as shown. With the highlighted side of the binding facing the quilt top, bind the edges of the quilt. Make sure the raw edges of the leaves and stem are covered by the binding.

1¼"   ½"   ½"

2. Appliqué the flower to the top of the stem. Fold and twist the leaves as desired and tack them in place.

3. Referring to "Couching Threads for Embellishment" (page 15), twist the green embellishing yarn and couch it to the bottom edge of the quilt to form the grass. Couch the trim piece over the top of the yarn. Stab stitch the 15 orange seed beads to the trim piece.

Finished size: 6" x 7"

These flowers are so simple to make, you will be amazed! Simple folding techniques and orange highlights turn this project into a real winner.

folded-petal
DAFFODILS

materials

2 pieces, 7" x 8", of blue fabric for background and backing

2 strips, 2¼" x 42", of yellow fabric for flowers

¼ yard of green fabric for stems and leaves

1 strip, 2½" x 42", of yellow fabric for binding

7" x 8" piece of thin, dense batting

Sewing thread to match fabrics

¼ yard of orange embellishing yarn

¼ yard of green eyelash yarn

3 yellow drop beads, size 4.5 mm

Orange oil pastel stick

Water-soluble fabric glue

Stencil brush

¼" bias-tape maker

making the quilt top

Unlike a standard appliqué quilt, this project requires that you quilt the quilt before adding the appliquéd flowers. Work through the following steps, referring to "Basic Quilt Construction" (page 6) as needed.

1. Layer the backing, batting, and background pieces.

2. Baste and quilt the layers, and then square the quilt to 6" x 7". Don't bind the quilt yet.

making the flowers

1. Crosscut the yellow 2¼" x 42" strips into 18 squares, 2¼" x 2¼".

2. Thread a hand-sewing needle with thread to match the yellow fabric. Referring to "Making Double-Folded Prairie Point Flowers" (page 13), fold the squares into double-folded prairie points. Join six petals, pulling the thread to gather the petals slightly. Stitch through the petals several times to lock the flower shape; knot the thread on the back of the flower. Make three flowers.

Make 3.

3. From the remainder of the yellow 2¼"-wide strip, cut a 2¼" x 11¼" piece. Press under a ¼" hem along both long sides of the piece. Press the piece in half lengthwise, wrong sides together. The piece should now measure ⅞" x 11¼". Rub the stencil brush over the orange oil pastel stick and then brush a ¼"-wide band of color along both sides of the fold.

4. Crosscut the painted strip into three 3¾"-long segments. Press under a ¼" hem on one end of each section. With right sides out, loop the raw edge of each strip around and into the finished edge of the strip. Use matching thread to blind-stitch the seam.

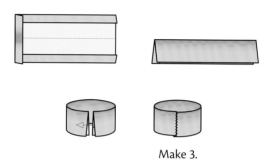

Make 3.

5. Use a running stitch to gather the bottom edge of each strip tightly to form a cup shape. Pass the needle through the bottom edge several times to lock the shape; knot the thread. Use the oil pastel stick and the stencil brush to add highlights to the center of each flower cup.

6. Use matching thread to blindstitch a cup to the center of each flower, making sure to cover all the raw edges of the flower. Stitch through the flower and cup several times to lock the shape; knot the thread but don't cut it yet. Push the needle up through the center of the flower and stab stitch a drop bead to the center of the flower, pulling the thread slightly to nestle the bead into the flower. Pass the needle back through the center of the flower to the back of the flower, and then knot and cut the thread. Make three flowers.

making the leaves and stems

1. Referring to "Basic Leaves" (page 10), cut two 6" x 11" strips from the green fabric and make five leaves as shown. (You will not need to crease the strip and will be stitching across its entire width.) Each leaf shape should measure about ½" wide at the bottom and 5½" high. Cut out the leaves and turn them right side out, finger-pressing them into shape.

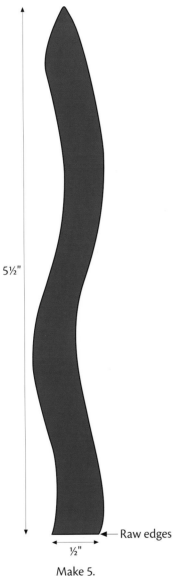

5½"

½"

← Raw edges

Make 5.

2. Referring to "Making Bias Tape" (page 9), use the remainder of the green fabric to make three 6"-long pieces of ¼"-wide bias tape. Refer to the quilt photo (page 34) to glue-baste the stems to the prepared background fabric, aligning one raw edge of each stem with the bottom raw edge of the quilt. Appliqué the stems in place. Glue-baste the bottom of the leaves to the quilt, aligning the leaf raw edges with the bottom raw edge of the quilt.

3. Referring to "Binding the Quilt" (page 8), use the yellow 2½" x 42" strip to make the binding and finish the edges of the quilt. Make sure the raw edges of the leaves and stems are covered by the binding.

finishing

Refer to the quilt photo as needed.

1. Appliqué the flowers to the tops of the stems. Fold and twist the leaves as desired and tack them in place.

2. Referring to "Couching Threads for Embellishment" (page 15), twist the orange and green yarns together and couch the yarns along the bottom of the stems to form the grass, leaving the ends to dangle for added texture.

Finished size: 6½" x 10½"

This flower has a simple name, but don't let that fool you—with

the added trim and beads, its appearance is anything but plain.

Add a butterfly to the grouping for a touch of whimsy.

folded-petal
FLOWERS

materials

2 pieces, 7½" x 11½", of dark blue fabric for background and backing

2 strips, 2½" x 42", of orange fabric for flowers and binding

¼ yard of green fabric for stems and leaves

Scrap of fabric with butterfly motif

Scrap of fabric that matches or contrasts with butterfly motif

7½" x 11½" piece of thin, dense batting

Sewing thread to match fabrics

1½" of black embellishing thread for butterfly antennae

½ yard of green eyelash yarn for grass

¼ yard of orange brush fringe for flower centers

3 black tri-beads for flower centers

3 orange seed beads, size 6/0, for flower centers

7 green seed beads, size 10/0, for butterfly body

1 green seed bead, size 6/0, for butterfly head

2 red seed beads, size 10/0, for butterfly antenna accents

Scrap of fusible web

Embellishing glue

Water-soluble fabric glue

¼" bias-tape maker

making the quilt top

Unlike a standard appliqué quilt, this quilt requires that you quilt and bind the quilt top before adding the appliquéd flowers. Work through the following steps, referring to "Basic Quilt Construction" (page 6) as needed.

1. Layer the backing, batting, and background pieces.

2. Baste and quilt the layers, and then square the quilt to 6½" x 10½".

3. Use one of the orange 2½" x 42" strips to make the binding and finish the edges of the quilt.

making the flowers

1. Crosscut the remaining orange 2½" x 42" strip into 15 squares, 2½" x 2½". Cut the orange brush fringe into three 1"-long pieces.

2. Referring to "Making Double-Folded Prairie Point Flowers" (page 13), fold the orange squares from step 1 into double-folded prairie points.

3. Thread a hand-sewing needle with thread to match the fabric. Join five petals, pulling the thread slightly to gather the petals into a ring; don't knot the thread.

4. Roll one piece of brush fringe into a tight roll and insert it into the center of the petals. Pull the thread tightly to gather the flower petals around the trim. Stitch through the flower petals and the trim to lock the flower shape; knot the thread but don't cut it. Push the needle up through the center of the flower, add one tri-bead and one orange seed bead to the needle, and then push the needle back through the center of the flower and knot it on the back; cut the thread.

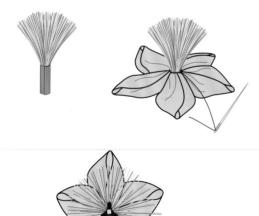

5. Repeat steps 3 and 4 to make a total of three flowers.

making the leaves and stems

1. Referring to "Basic Leaves" (page 10), cut two 6" x 9" pieces from the green fabric and make three leaves. (You will not need to crease the strip and will stitch across the width of the pieces.) Each leaf should measure 1" at the bottom and 5½" high. Cut out the leaves and turn them right side out, finger-pressing them into shape.

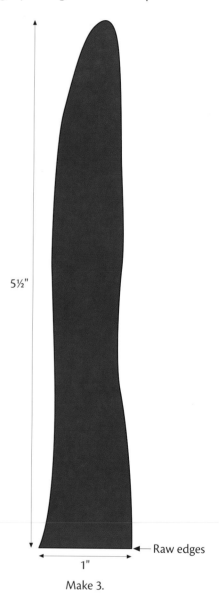

5½"

← Raw edges

1"

Make 3.

2. Turn up a ¼" hem around the bottom of each leaf; finger-press it in place. Use matching green thread to stitch through the center of each leaf and topstitch around the edge.

Start stitching here.

End stitching here.

3. Using the remaining green fabric, refer to "Making Bias Tape" (page 9) to make 22" of ¼"-wide bias tape. Refer to the quilt photo (page 38) to cut the strips into three stems of varying lengths. Glue-baste the stems to the prepared background fabric. Appliqué the stems in place. Tack the leaves to the bottoms of the stems, folding and twisting them as desired.

making the butterfly

1. Follow the manufacturer's instructions to fuse the scrap of fabric with the butterfly printed on it to the matching or contrasting fabric, right sides out. Cut out the butterfly motif and curl up the wings for added texture. Tack the butterfly to the background fabric, leaving the wings unstitched so the butterfly is three-dimensional.

2. Use the embellishing glue to attach one red seed bead to each end of the black embellishing thread to make the antennae; allow the glue to dry.

3. Stitch the seven small green seed beads to the center of the butterfly, end to end, to form the body. Add the large green seed bead to the top of the body for the head; do not clip your thread yet. Wrap the thread around the center of the antennae, and then bring the needle back through the head bead. Push the needle to the back of the quilt and knot the thread.

finishing

Refer to the quilt photo as needed.

1. Appliqué the flowers to the tops of the stems.

2. Referring to "Couching Threads for Embellishment" (page 15), couch the green eyelash yarn along the bottom of the stems to form the grass, leaving the ends of the embellishing thread to dangle for added texture.

Finished size: 8½" x 10"

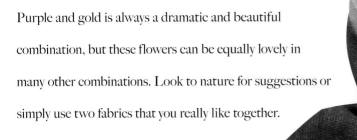

Purple and gold is always a dramatic and beautiful combination, but these flowers can be equally lovely in many other combinations. Look to nature for suggestions or simply use two fabrics that you really like together.

TWO-TONE FOLDED-PETAL flowers

materials

2 pieces, 9½" x 11", of mottled light yellow fabric for background and backing

1 strip, 1" x 42", of golden yellow fabric for accent trim

1 strip, 2½" x 42", of purple fabric for binding

3 strips, 1½" x 42", of purple fabric for flowers

3 strips, 1¾" x 42", of golden yellow fabric for flowers

1 strip, 2" x 14", of golden yellow fabric for flower centers

¼ yard of green fabric for leaves and vine

9½" x 11" piece of thin, dense batting

Sewing thread to match fabrics

3 yards of light purple embellishing yarn

7 light purple seed beads, size 6/0

63 dark purple seed beads, size 10/0

Template material

Water-soluble fabric glue

¼" bias-tape maker

making the quilt top

Unlike a standard appliqué quilt, this project requires that you quilt and bind the quilt before adding the appliquéd flowers. Work through the following steps, referring to "Basic Quilt Construction" (page 6) as needed.

1. Layer the backing, batting, and background pieces.

2. Baste and quilt the layers, and then square the quilt to 8½" x 10".

3. Using the golden yellow 1" x 42" strip, refer to "Adding Accent Trim" (page 7) to add the accent strips to the quilt. Use the purple 2½" x 42" strip to make the binding and finish the edges of the quilt.

making the flowers

1. Layer a purple 1½" x 42" strip and a golden yellow 1¾" x 42" strip right sides together with one long edge aligned. Sew ¼" from the long, aligned edges. Press the seam allowance toward the purple strip. Repeat to make a total of three strip sets.

Make 3.

2. Fold each strip set in half lengthwise, wrong sides together, aligning the long, raw edges. The yellow strips will be wider than the purple strips. Press the folded edge of the strip sets.

3. Crosscut the strip sets into 35 segments, 2¾" wide.

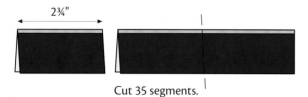

Cut 35 segments.

4. Referring to "Making Double-Folded Prairie Point Flowers" (page 13), fold the segments into double-folded prairie points with the golden yellow fabric on the inside of the folds.

5. Thread a hand-sewing needle with thread to match the purple fabric. Join five petals, pulling the thread to gather the petals slightly. Stitch through the petals several times to lock the flower shape; knot the thread on the back of the flower. Make seven flowers.

Make 7.

6. Use the pattern on page 45 to make a flower center template from the template material. Use the template to cut seven circles from the golden yellow 2" x 14" strip. Referring to "Basic Yo-Yos" (page 15), make seven tightly gathered yo-yos for the flower centers.

7. Using thread to match the golden yellow fabric, blindstitch a yo-yo to the center of a flower, making sure all the raw edges of the flower are covered; knot your thread but do not cut it. Push

the needle up through the center of the flower and stab stitch one light purple seed bead in the center of the flower; push the needle to the back of the flower and knot the thread, but do not cut it. Bring the needle back up through the center of the flower and stab stitch nine of the dark purple seed beads around the light purple bead to form the flower center. Push the needle to the back of the flower and knot and cut the thread. Repeat for all seven flowers.

making the stems and leaves

1. Referring to "Making Bias Tape" (page 9), use the green fabric to make 22" of ¼"-wide bias tape. Use the 6½"-diameter vine placement pattern on page 45 to make a template from the template material. Center the template on the prepared quilt top and mark around it. Glue-baste the green bias tape to the marked line, positioning the ends where a flower will cover them; trim the excess. Appliqué the bias tape in place, making sure your stitches don't go through to the backing fabric.

2. Referring to "Basic Leaves" (page 10), use the remaining green fabric to cut two 4" x 20" strips and make 17 leaves. Each leaf should measure 1" wide at the bottom and 1½" high. Cut out the leaves and turn them right side out, finger-pressing them into shape. There is no need to turn up a hem on the bottom edge of the leaves because they will be covered by the flowers.

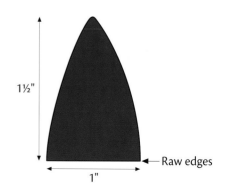

1½"

1"

← Raw edges

3. Thread a hand-sewing needle with thread to match the green fabric. Blindstitch two leaves to the back of four of the flowers. Blindstitch three leaves to the back of the remaining three flowers.

Blindstitch 2 leaves to the back of 4 flowers and 3 leaves to the back of 3 flowers.

finishing

Refer to the quilt photo on page 42 as needed.

1. Referring to "Couching Threads for Embellishment" (page 15), couch the light purple embellishing yarn to the prepared background fabric.

2. Position the flowers over the vine and appliqué them to the background fabric.

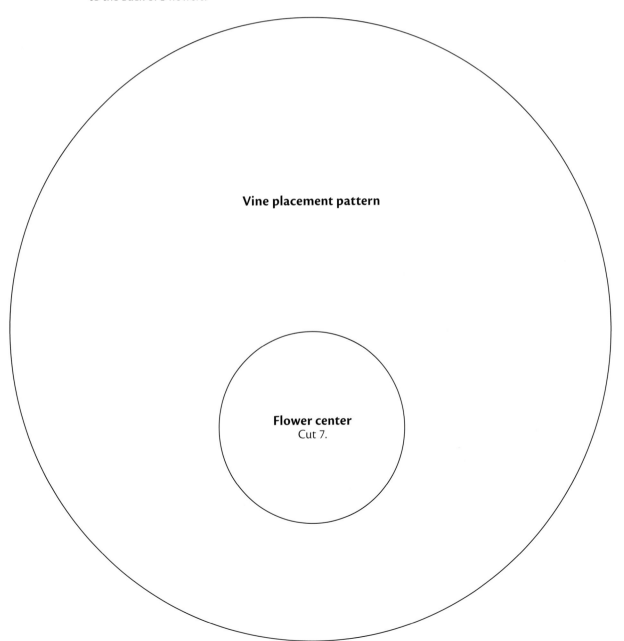

Vine placement pattern

Flower center
Cut 7.

The rose is a perennial favorite in the garden, not only for its beauty but also for its lovely fragrance. These sweet pink rosebuds are so lifelike, you can almost smell them! But don't limit yourself to just pink—make them in a rainbow of colors to give as gifts.

two-tone
ROSEBUDS

materials

2 pieces, 6½" x 9", of mottled light pink fabric for background and backing

1 strip, 2½" x 42", of bright pink fabric for binding

1 strip, 1¼" x 42", of bright pink fabric for flower buds

1 strip, 1" x 42", of medium pink fabric for flower buds

2 strips, 2½" x 24", of green fabric for calyxes

2 strips, 4" x 20", of green fabric for leaves

6½" x 9" piece of thin, dense batting

Sewing thread to match fabrics

2 yards of green embellishing yarn

4" x 20" strip of fusible web

Template material

making the quilt top

Unlike a standard appliqué quilt, this project requires that you quilt and bind the quilt before adding the appliquéd flowers. Work through the following steps, referring to "Basic Quilt Construction" (page 6) as needed.

1. Layer the backing, batting, and background pieces.

2. Baste and quilt the layers, and then square the quilt to 5½" x 8".

3. Use the 2½" x 42" strip of bright pink fabric to make the binding and finish the edges of the quilt.

making the flowers

1. Layer the bright pink 1¼" x 42" strip with the medium pink 1" x 42" strip, right sides together with one long edge aligned. Sew ¼" from the long, aligned edges to make a strip set. Press the seam allowance toward the medium pink strip.

2. Fold the strip set in half lengthwise, wrong sides together, aligning the long, raw edges. The bright pink strip will be wider than the medium pink strip. Press the folded edge of the strip set.

3. Crosscut the strip set into 23 segments, 2" wide.

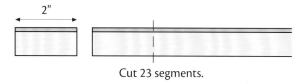

Cut 23 segments.

4. Thread a hand-sewing needle with thread to match the medium pink fabric. Fold the right corner down first, with the bright pink on the inside of the fold; then fold the left side over the right side. Stitch through the bottom edge of the bud, pulling the thread tightly to gather. Stitch through the bud several times to lock the shape; knot and cut the thread. Make 23 buds.

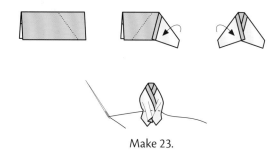

Make 23.

making the leaves and calyxes

1. Referring to "Fused Leaves" (page 11), layer the fusible-web strip between the two green 4" x 20" strips and fuse them together, following the manu-facturer's instructions. Use the patterns at right to make leaf templates from the template material. Mark 12 large leaves and 6 small leaves on the fused fabric. Topstitch through the center of each leaf and then zigzag stitch around the outer edges. Cut out the leaves and then press each one to set the stitching.

2. Referring to "Making a Calyx" (page 12), use the two green 2½" x 24" strips to make 23 hump shapes to use as calyxes for the flower buds. Each calyx shape should measure ½" wide at the bottom and ¾" high. Cut out the calyxes and turn them right side out. Turn up a ⅛" hem around the bottom of each calyx; finger-press it in place.

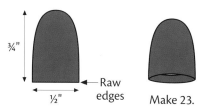

¾"

½"

Raw edges

Make 23.

3. Thread a hand-sewing needle with thread to match the green fabric. Insert a rosebud into each calyx, making sure all the raw edges of the bud are covered by the calyx. Blindstitch the calyxes to the flower buds, pulling the thread slightly to gather. Stitch through the calyx and bud several times to lock the shape; knot the thread on the back of the flower bud. Make 23 flower buds.

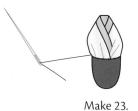

Make 23.

finishing

Refer to the quilt photo on page 46 as needed.

1. Referring to "Couching Threads for Embellishment" (page 15), couch the green embellishing yarn to the background fabric in a loose oval shape to act as stems for the buds and leaves.

2. Appliqué the flower buds to the background fabric.

3. Tack the leaves to the background fabric.

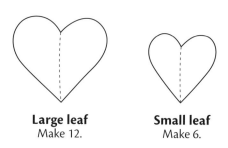

Large leaf
Make 12.

Small leaf
Make 6.

I have always wanted a koi pond in my backyard, but I really don't want to deal with all the stuff that goes along with owning one. So . . . I made one for indoors! Now anyone can have a koi pond. I think it looks fabulous on the wall or on a table.

WATER lilies

materials

1 piece, 22" x 22", of fabric with water-and-koi motif for background

1 piece, 22" x 22", of blue batik for backing

¼ yard of rock print

3 strips, 2¼" x 42", of white fabric for large flower petals

2 strips, 1¾" x 42", of white fabric for medium flower petals

2 strips, 1½" x 42", of white fabric for small flower petals

¼ yard of green fabric for leaves

2 strips, 2½" x 42", of black fabric for binding

22" x 22" piece of thin, dense batting

9" x 22" piece of thin, dense batting for stuffing rocks

¼ yard of sewable fusible web

Sewing thread to match fabrics

1 yard of green embellishing yarn for moss

¼ yard of bright green embellishing yarn for floating greenery

1 yard of bright yellow embellishing yarn for flower centers

100 iridescent purple seed beads, size 10/0

100 iridescent yellow seed beads, size 10/0

Purple oil pastel stick

Template material

Small stencil brush

Finished size: 21" x 21"

making the quilt top

Unlike a standard appliqué quilt, this project requires that you quilt the quilt top before adding the appliquéd flowers. Work through the following steps, referring to "Basic Quilt Construction" (page 6) as needed.

1. Layer the blue batik backing piece, the 22" x 22" piece of batting, and the background piece.

2. Baste and quilt the layers, but do not square or bind the quilt yet.

making the rock border

1. With right sides together, fold the piece of rock fabric in half crosswise. Place the 9" x 22" piece of batting under the folded fabric. Stitch through the layers to create nine rock shapes that are approximately 4½" wide at the base and 2½" high, leaving the bottom edge open. Vary the shapes for interest. Cut out the rock shapes ¼" from the stitching lines and turn them right side out; press them into shape.

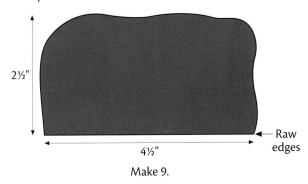

Make 9.

2. Pin the rock shapes around the outside edges of the quilt, aligning the raw edges of the rocks with the outer edges of the quilt. Angle the rocks at the corners. Quilt the rock shapes to the background fabric, using a smaller rock motif and leaving the

finished edges of the rocks unquilted for added texture.

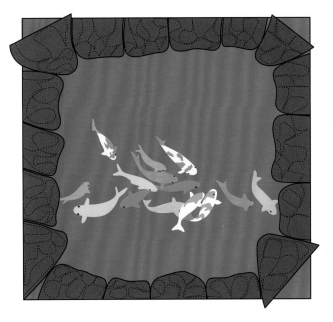

3. Trim the edges of the quilt to look like a pond with rounded corners and wavy sides. Referring to "Binding the Quilt" (page 8), use the black 2½" x 42" strips to make the binding and finish the edges of the quilt.

making the flowers

1. Crosscut the white 2¼" x 42" strips into 35 squares, 2¼" x 2¼", for the large flowers. Crosscut the white 1¾" x 42" strips into 35 squares, 1¾" x 1¾", for the medium flowers. Crosscut the white 1½" x 42" strips into 38 squares, 1½" x 1½", for the small flowers.

2. Fold each square in half, wrong sides together; finger-press the folds. Rub the stencil brush over the purple oil pastel stick and then brush the fold on one side of the squares with the paint as shown.

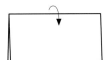 

3. Referring to "Making Double-Folded Prairie Point Flowers" (page 13), finish folding the squares, with the purple highlight on the inside of the folds; crease the folds.

4. Thread a hand-sewing needle with white thread. Join seven large folded squares, pulling the thread to gather the petals slightly. Stitch through the petals several times to lock the flower shape; knot the thread on the back of the flower. Make five large flowers. Repeat with the medium and small folded squares to make five medium and five small flowers. You will have three small folded squares left over for making the buds.

Make 5 large, 5 medium,
and 5 small flowers.

5. With the needle still threaded with white thread, layer one medium flower over a large flower, offsetting the petals. Stitch the two flowers together. Layer a small flower over the medium flower, once again offsetting the petals, and stitch through all three flowers to join them. Make five flowers.

Make 5.

6. Cut the yellow embellishing yarn into five 7"-long pieces. Thread a hand-sewing needle with thread to match the yellow embellishing yarn. Wrap one piece of the embellishing yarn around your finger three to four times, and then twist the loops into a figure-eight shape. Place the twisted loop of embellishing yarn on the center of a flower and stab stitch the center of the loops down to cover the flower center. Cut the loops. Repeat for each flower.

7. Thread a hand-sewing needle with white thread. Come up from the bottom of the flower into the flower center; thread four iridescent purple beads onto the needle. Pass the needle back through the first three beads, and reinsert the needle into the flower right next to the spot where it first emerged; knot the thread on the back of the flower but do not cut it. (Knotting the thread after each stack of beads keeps the beads tight on the thread, and if the thread breaks you only have to rethread one stack.) Repeat the process with the yellow beads. Make five stacks of each color bead in the center of all five flowers.

Make 5 stacks of purple beads
and 5 stacks of yellow beads
for each flower.

making the calyx and leaves

1. Referring to "Making a Calyx" (page 12), use the green fabric to make one calyx that is ¾" wide at the bottom and ¾" high. Cut out the calyx and turn it right side out; finger-press it into shape. Turn under a ⅛" hem along the bottom edge of the calyx and finger-press it in place.

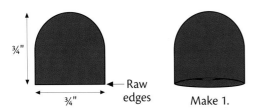

¾"

¾"

← Raw edges

Make 1.

2. Thread a hand-sewing needle with white thread. Join the remaining three small double-folded prairie points along the lower edges as you did for the flowers, pulling the thread to gather the petals slightly. Insert the flower bud into the prepared calyx. Make sure all the raw edges of the bud are covered by the calyx. Thread a hand-sewing needle with thread to match the calyx. Blindstitch the calyx to the bud along the folded edge, pulling the thread slightly to gather.

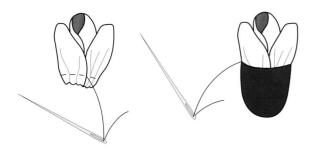

3. Use the patterns on page 54 to make templates for the large, medium, and small leaves from the template material. Refer to "Fused Leaves" (page 11) and use the templates, the remaining green fabric, and the fusible web to make five large leaves, five medium leaves, and one small leaf. Use matching green thread to topstitch the veins on each leaf, following the patterns. Zigzag stitch around the outer edge of each leaf. Cut out the leaves and then press each one to set the stitching.

finishing

Refer to the quilt photo on page 50 as needed.

1. Tack the leaves to the background fabric, adding a few tucks and folds as desired for added texture.

2. Appliqué the flowers and the bud to the background fabric.

3. Cut the green embellishing yarn into small pieces. Referring to "Couching Threads for Embellishment" (page 15), couch the pieces to the rocks to form moss.

4. Cut the bright green embellishing yarn into small pieces and couch them to the water to form the floating greenery.

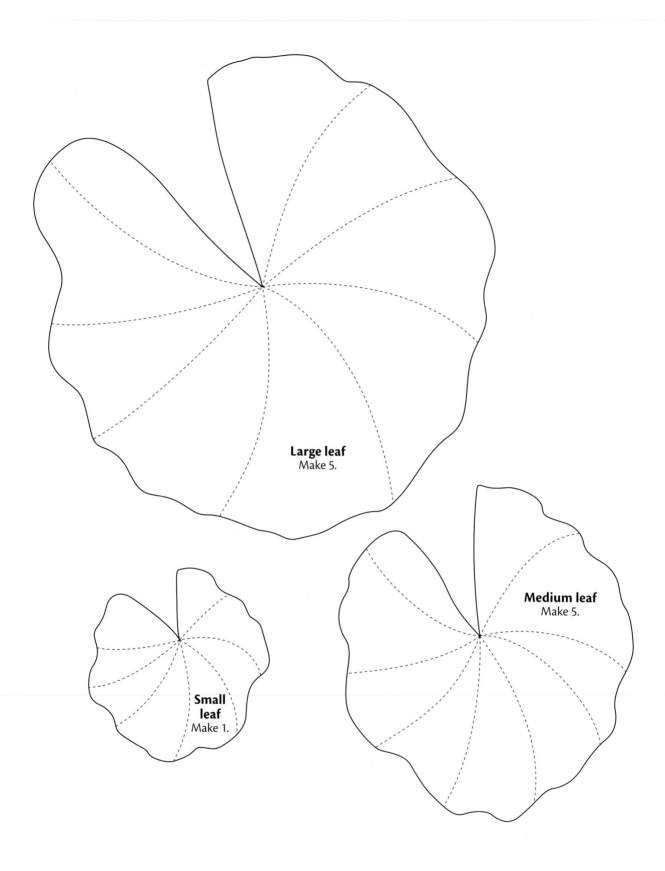

Large leaf
Make 5.

Medium leaf
Make 5.

**Small
leaf**
Make 1.

The multicolored batik and fun trims make this quilt look like a party. Easy and quick to make, these flowers would be great for adding cheer to even the cloudiest day.

mardi gras FLOWERS

materials

2 pieces, 8" x 7", of light multicolored fabric for background and backing

5 strips, 1½" x 21", of bright multicolored batik for flowers

⅛ yard of green fabric for stems and leaves

1 strip, 2½" x 42", of multicolored batik for binding

8" x 7" piece of thin, dense batting

Sewing thread to match fabrics

1½ yards of multicolored embellishing yarn for flower centers

½ yard of green eyelash yarn for grass

¼ yard of multicolored ladder yarn for grass accent

15 clear drop beads, size 4.5 mm

4" x 8" piece of sewable fusible web

Water-soluble fabric glue

Template material

¼" bias-tape maker

making the Quilt Top

Unlike a standard appliqué quilt, this project requires that you quilt the quilt top before adding the appliquéd flowers. Work through the following steps, referring to "Basic Quilt Construction" (page 6) as needed.

1. Layer the backing, batting, and background pieces.

2. Baste and quilt the layers, and then square the quilt to 7" x 5¾". Don't bind the quilt yet.

making the flowers

1. Fold each bright batik 1½" x 21" strip in half lengthwise, wrong sides together; press.

2. Using a hand-sewing needle with a double strand of coordinating thread, start at the fold of a strip from step 1 and sew a running stitch to the raw edge of the strip, stitching through both layers. Continue stitching along the raw edge until you reach the other end, and then stitch back up to the fold.

Start stitching.

Finished size: 7" x 5¾"

3. Pull the thread to gather the strip. The fabric will curl into a spiral; adjust the gathers. Do not knot the thread yet. With a second needle threaded with a single strand of matching thread, whipstitch the raw edges together at the beginning (center) of the spiral. Continue stitching along the raw edges of the strip, adjusting the gathers until you have all the "petals" joined. Knot both threads when you are pleased with the look of your flower.

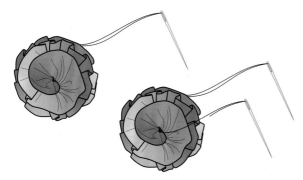

4. Repeat steps 2 and 3 to make five flowers.

5. Cut the multicolored embellishing yarn into five 10"-long pieces. For each flower, wrap the embellishing yarn around one finger six to eight times, and then twist the loops into a figure-eight shape. Place the twisted loop of embellishing yarn on the center of one flower and stab stitch the center of the loops down to cover the flower center.

6. Stab stitch three drop beads in the center of each flower; knot the thread on the back of the flower after each bead to hold the bead tight against the embellishing thread.

making the stems and leaves

1. Referring to "Making Bias Tape" (page 9), use the green fabric to make 20" of ¼"-wide bias tape. Refer to the quilt photo at left to cut the strips into five stems of varying lengths. Glue-baste the stems to the prepared background fabric, aligning one raw edge of each stem with the bottom raw edge of the quilt. Appliqué the stems to the background fabric.

2. Referring to "Binding the Quilt" (page 8), use the multicolored batik 2½" x 42" strip to make the binding and finish the edges of the quilt. Make sure the raw edges of the stems are covered by the binding.

3. Cut two 4" x 8" strips from the remaining green fabric. Use the patterns below to make templates for the large, medium, and small leaves from the template material. Refer to "Fused Leaves" (page 11) and use the templates, the green strips, and the fusible web to make three large leaves, four medium leaves, and two small leaves. Use matching green thread to topstitch the side and center veins on each leaf and then zigzag stitch around the outer edges. Cut out the leaves and then press each one to set the stitching.

finishing

Refer to the quilt photo on page 56 as needed.

1. Tack the leaves to the stems.

2. Appliqué the flowers to the tops of the stems.

3. Cut the multicolored ladder yarn into four equal pieces. Stitch the pieces to the bottom edge of the quilt. Twist the green eyelash yarn together. Referring to "Couching Threads for Embellishment" (page 15), couch the yarn to the bottom edge of the quilt to form the grass, leaving the ends to dangle for added texture.

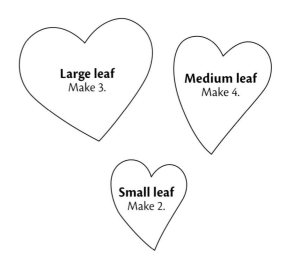

Large leaf
Make 3.

Medium leaf
Make 4.

Small leaf
Make 2.

Finished size: 9" x 8"

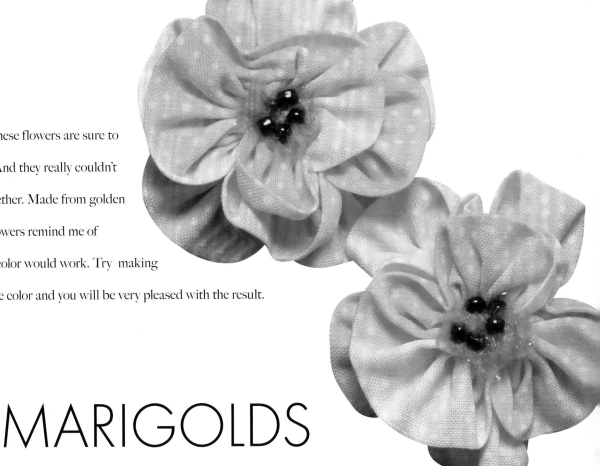

Sunny and bright, these flowers are sure to become a favorite! And they really couldn't be easier to put together. Made from golden yellow fabric, the flowers remind me of marigolds, but any color would work. Try making some in your favorite color and you will be very pleased with the result.

MARIGOLDS

materials

2 pieces, 10" x 9", of dark purple fabric for background and backing

8 strips, 1½" x 24", of mottled yellow fabric for flowers

¼ yard of green fabric for stems and leaves

1 strip, 2½" x 42", of mottled yellow fabric for binding

10" x 9" piece of thin, dense batting

Sewing thread to match fabrics

2 yards of orange embellishing yarn for flower centers

½ yard of green eyelash yarn for grass

40 black seed beads, size 10/0

Water-soluble fabric glue

¼" bias-tape maker

making the quilt top

Unlike a standard appliqué quilt, this project requires that you quilt the quilt before adding the appliquéd flowers. Work through the following steps, referring to "Basic Quilt Construction" (page 6) as needed.

1. Layer the backing, batting, and background pieces.

2. Baste and quilt the layers, and then square the quilt to 9" x 8". Don't bind the quilt yet.

making the flowers

1. Fold each mottled yellow 1½" x 24" strip in half lengthwise, wrong sides together; press.

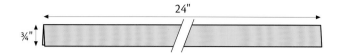

2. Thread a hand-sewing needle with a double strand of thread that matches the yellow fabric. Starting at the fold of a strip from step 1, sew a running stitch to the raw edge of the strip, stitching through both layers and at a slight angle. Following the diagram, take five stitches across the raw edge, then three stitches up and three down to make a zigzag. Repeat this series 10 more times, gradually increasing the number of stitches across the raw edge for the next three repeats until you are up to 10 stitches. Continue taking 10 stitches across the raw edge for the remainder of the repeats. Stitch back up to the folded edge.

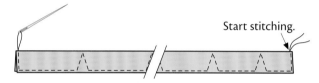

Start stitching.

3. Pull the thread to gather the strip. The strip will curl around on itself; adjust the gathers until you have a nice shape for the flower. Do not knot the thread yet. With a second needle threaded with a single strand of matching thread, whipstitch the raw edges together at the beginning (center) of the spiral. Continue stitching along the raw edges of the strip, adjusting the gathers until you have all the "petals" joined. Knot both threads when you are pleased with the look of your flower.

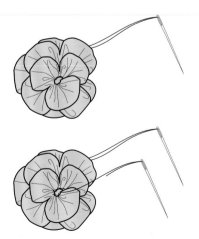

4. Repeat steps 2 and 3 to make eight flowers.

5. Cut the orange embellishing thread into eight 9"-long pieces. For each flower, wrap one piece of embellishing thread around your finger six to eight times, and then twist the loops into a figure-eight shape. Thread a hand-sewing needle with thread to match the embellishing thread. Place the twisted loop of embellishing thread on the center of one flower and stab stitch the center of the loop down to cover the flower center.

6. Stab stitch five black seed beads in the center of each flower; knot the thread on the back of the flower.

making the stems and leaves

1. Referring to "Making Bias Tape" (page 9), use the green fabric to make 30" of ¼"-wide bias tape. Refer to the quilt photo (page 58) to cut the strips into eight stems of varying lengths. Glue-baste the stems to the prepared background fabric, aligning one raw end of the stems with the bottom raw edge of the quilt. Appliqué the stems to the background fabric.

2. From the remaining green fabric, cut two 6" x 9" strips. Layer the fabric right sides together. Referring to "Basic Leaves" (page 10), make nine leaves. (You will not need to crease the strip and will stitch across its entire width.) Each leaf shape should measure about ¾" wide at the bottom and 5" to 5½" high. Cut out the leaves and turn them right side out, finger-pressing them into shape.

5" to 5½"

¾"

Raw edges

Make 9.

3. Use matching green thread to stitch through the middle of each leaf and topstitch around the outside edge. Press the leaves to set the stitching. Refer to the quilt photo (page 58) to glue-baste the bottom edge of the leaves to the bottom edge of the quilt.

Start stitching here.

End stitching here.

finishing

Refer to the quilt photo as needed.

1. Referring to "Binding the Quilt" (page 8), use the mottled yellow 2½" x 42" strip to make the binding and finish the edges of the quilt. Make sure the raw edges of the stems and leaves are covered by the binding.

2. Twist and fold the leaves as desired and then tack them in place.

3. Appliqué the flowers to the tops of the stems.

4. Referring to "Couching Threads for Embellishment" (page 15), twist the green eyelash yarn and couch the yarn along the bottom of the stems to form the grass, leaving the ends to dangle for added texture.

These flowers are made using a ruching stitch called the heart-monitor stitch. This stitch makes an amazing flower! Classic style and awesome texture really fill up the woven basket with charm. If you don't want to make the woven basket, use a basket-print fabric instead. Either way, you will have a classic quilt you'll want to share.

PINK clouds

materials

2 pieces, 8" x 9", of light yellow fabric for background and backing

1 strip, 2½" x 42", of gradated pink fabric for binding

5 strips, 1½" x 42", of gradated pink fabric for large flowers

1 strip, 1½" x 21", of gradated pink fabric for medium flower

2 strips, 1½" x 11", of gradated pink fabric for small flowers

2 strips, 4" x 22", of green fabric for leaves

8" x 9" piece of thin, dense batting

Sewing thread to match fabrics

2 yards of dark purple embellishing yarn for flower centers

10 yards of green embellishing yarn for basket

10 yards of tan embellishing yarn for basket

6 yards of white embellishing yarn for basket

20 seed beads, size 6/0

5" x 4" piece of sturdy cardboard

Water-soluble fabric glue

making the quilt top

Unlike a standard appliqué quilt, this project requires that you quilt and bind the quilt before adding the appliquéd flowers. Work through the following steps, referring to "Basic Quilt Construction" (page 6) as needed.

1. Layer the backing, batting, and background pieces.

2. Baste and quilt the layers, and then square the quilt to 7" x 8".

3. Use the gradated pink 2½" x 42" strip to make the binding and finish the edges of the quilt.

making the basket

This is a very simple form of weaving; the basket is woven on a cardboard loom. I learned to weave like this in Girl Scouts, and it's just as much fun now as it was then. You simply wrap the embellishing yarn around a piece of cardboard and weave the horizontal threads (weft) in a pattern between the vertical threads (warp).

1. Cut notches ¼" apart into the top and bottom of the cardboard piece. (I used a pinking rotary-cutting blade to cut the notches in my cardboard.) You should have at least 18 "valleys" on each side.

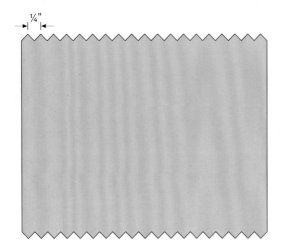

2. Wrap the tan yarn around the cardboard from notch to notch, going from front to back. These threads are called the warp.

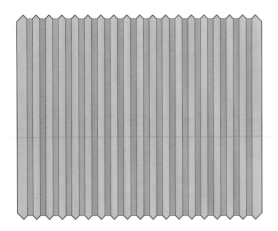

3. On the back of the cardboard piece, loop one end of the green yarn around the first warp thread. On the front of the cardboard, weave the green yarn over and under the warp threads the length of the cardboard. When you reach the end, loop back and make a second row. Continue in this manner to weave a total of four rows with the green yarn. Secure the yarn on the back of the piece at the end of the row.

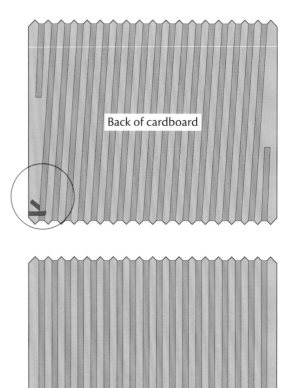

Back of cardboard

4. In the same manner, weave the remaining rows in the following order with the embellishing yarns indicated. Secure the yarns at the beginning and end of every color change.

    White: 1 row

    Green: 5 rows

    White: 3 rows

    Green: 9 rows

    White: 5 rows

    Green: 12 rows.

5. Remove the woven piece from the cardboard. To do this, squeeze the middle of the cardboard piece at the top and bottom edges and pull the cardboard out through the vertical yarns at the top. Refer to the photo on page 62 to position the woven piece on the prepared background quilt; pin it in place. Tuck the loose warp (tan yarn) to the back of the basket. Tack the basket to the background, making sure you secure the middle of the basket and all of the sides.

6. From each of the tan, green, and white embellishing yarns, cut a 1-yard length. Knot the yarns together at one end, leaving about a 1" tail. Braid the yarns together. Beginning at the top center of the woven piece and leaving 2" to 3" hanging free, tack the braided length around the edges of the woven piece. When you reach the starting point, leave another 2" to 3" hanging free. Cut off any excess and knot the ends, leaving about a 1" tail unbraided.

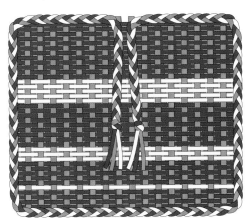

making the flowers

1. Fold each gradated pink 1½" x 42" strip in half lengthwise, wrong sides together; press. Repeat with the gradated pink 1½" x 21" and 1½" x 11" strips.

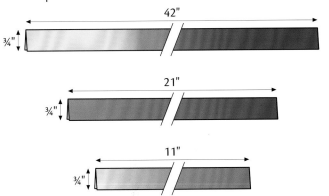

2. Thread a hand-sewing needle with a double strand of thread that matches the pink fabric. Starting at the folded edge of the 1½" x 42" strip, sew a running stitch to the raw edge of the strip, stitching through both layers. Following the diagram, take four stitches across the raw edge, then three stitches up and three down to make a zigzag, and then six more stitches across the raw edge. Continue the pattern across the length of the strip, taking eight stitches across the raw edge.

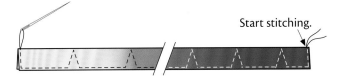

Start stitching.

3. Pull the thread to gather the strip. The strip will curl around itself; adjust the gathers until you have a nice shape for the flower. Do not knot the thread yet. With a second needle threaded with a single strand of matching thread, whipstitch the raw edges together at the beginning (center) of the spiral. Continue stitching along the raw edges of the strip; adjust the gathers until you have all the "petals" joined. Knot both threads when you are pleased with the look of your flower.

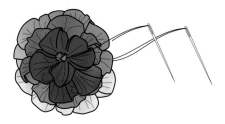

4. Repeat steps 2 and 3 with the remaining gradated pink strips to make a total of five large flowers, one medium flower, and two small flowers.

5. Cut the dark purple embellishing yarn into eight 9"-long pieces. Wrap one piece of embellishing yarn around one finger six to eight times, and then twist the loops into a figure-eight shape. Thread a hand-sewing needle with thread to match the embellishing yarn. Place the twisted loop of embellishing yarn on the center of one flower and stab stitch the center of the loops down to cover the flower center. Repeat for each flower.

6. Stab stitch three large seed beads in the center of each large flower and one bead in each of the two small flowers. Knot the thread on the back of the flower after each bead to hold the bead tight against the embellishing yarn.

making the leaves

Referring to "Basic Leaves" (page 10), use the green 4" x 22" strips to make 17 leaves. Each leaf should measure 1" wide at the bottom and 2" high. Cut out the leaves and turn them right side out, finger-pressing them into shape. Turn up a 1/8" hem around the bottom of each leaf and finger-press it in place. Use matching green thread to tightly gather the bottom of each leaf.

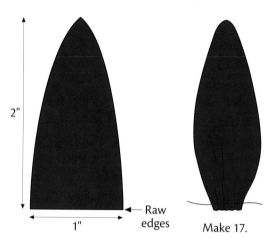

2"

1"

Raw edges

Make 17.

finishing

Refer to the quilt photo on page 62 as needed.

1. Appliqué the leaves to the background fabric.

2. Appliqué the flowers to the background fabric.

The larkspur is a wonderful flower, and making the fabric version couldn't be easier! These beautiful rosy-pink spikes seem to glisten like candles. I used a fabric with a wide stripe, which really added to the shading of the spikes. Any color combination or stripe pattern will work for these fabulous blooms!

RUCHED
larkspurs

materials

2 pieces, 5" x 7½", of light pink fabric for background and backing

5 strips, 1" x 16", of wide-striped pink fabric for flowers

⅛ yard of green fabric for stems and leaves

1 strip, 2½" x 42", of wide-striped pink fabric for binding

5" x 7½" piece of thin, dense batting

Sewing thread to match fabrics

¼ yard of green embellishing yarn for grass

Water-soluble fabric glue

½" bias-tape maker

¼" bias-tape maker

making the quilt top

Unlike a standard appliqué quilt, this project requires that you quilt the quilt before adding the appliquéd flowers. Work through the following steps, referring to "Basic Quilt Construction" (page 6) as needed.

1. Layer the backing, batting, and background pieces.

2. Baste and quilt the layers, and then square the quilt to 4" x 6½". Don't bind the quilt yet.

making the flowers

1. Referring to step 2 of "Making Bias Tape" (page 9), use the striped pink 1" x 16" strips to make five ½"-wide tape pieces.

2. Thread a hand-sewing needle with thread to match the pink fabric; knot the ends together. Press under a ⅛" hem at both ends of each tape piece. Insert the needle from the back side of the strip to the front at one end of the strip. Using a running stitch, sew across the hem to secure it. Sew an evenly spaced triangle pattern across about three-quarters of the strip as shown, and then start making the triangles and the distance between them narrower and narrower until you have stitched across the entire strip. When you get to the end of the strip, stitch across the hem to secure it.

Start stitching.

3. Pull the thread to gather the strip; adjust the gathers until you are pleased with the size and look of your flower. If necessary, zigzag stitch across the raw edges on the back of the flower to keep the raw edges from showing on the front of the flower; knot your thread on the back of the flower.

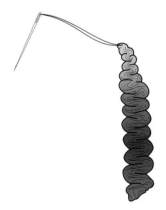

4. Repeat steps 2 and 3 to make a total of five flowers.

making the stems and leaves

1. Referring to "Making Bias Tape," use the green fabric to make 15" of ¼"-wide bias tape. Cut the strips into five stems of varying length.

2. Referring to the quilt photo at left as needed, glue-baste the stems to the prepared background fabric, aligning one raw end of the stems with the bottom raw edge of the quilt. Appliqué the stems to the background fabric.

3. Referring to "Basic Leaves" (page 10), cut two 4½" x 10" strips from the remaining green fabric and make nine leaves. Each leaf should measure ½" wide at the bottom and 2½" high. Cut out the leaves and turn them right side out, finger-pressing them into shape.

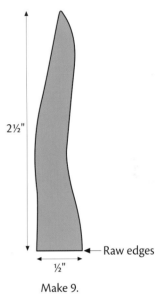

2½"

½"

Raw edges

Make 9.

4. Glue-baste the bottom edge of the leaves to the bottom edge of the quilt, aligning the raw edges.

5. Referring to "Binding the Quilt" (page 8), use the striped pink 2½" x 42" strip to make the binding and finish the edges of the quilt. Make sure the raw edges of the leaves and stems are covered by the binding.

finishing

Refer to the quilt photo at left as needed.

1. Appliqué the flowers to the tops of the stems.

2. Referring to "Couching Threads for Embellishment" (page 15), couch the green embellishing yarn along the bottom of the stems to form the grass, leaving the ends to dangle for added texture.

3. Twist and turn the leaves as desired and tack them in place.

Finished size: 6½" x 4"

These five little flowers are absolutely charming. Use a striped fabric for a flower with color variation, or make them from a solid fabric in your favorite color. They'll be fabulous no matter what you choose!

RUCHED mini flowers

materials

2 pieces, 7½" x 5", of light pink fabric for background and backing

5 strips, 1" x 6", of wide-striped pink fabric for flowers

⅛ yard of green fabric for stems and leaves

1 strip, 2½" x 42", of wide-striped pink fabric for binding

7½" x 5" piece of thin, dense batting

Sewing thread to match fabrics

25" of pink embellishing thread for flower centers

⅓ yard of green embellishing yarn for grass

15 white drop beads, size 4.5 mm

Water-soluble fabric glue

¼" bias-tape maker

making the quilt top

Unlike a standard appliqué quilt, this project requires that you quilt the quilt before adding the appliquéd flowers. Work through the following steps, referring to "Basic Quilt Construction" (page 6) as needed.

1. Layer the backing, batting, and background pieces.

2. Baste and quilt the layers, and then square the quilt to 6½" x 4". Don't bind the quilt yet.

making the flowers

1. Referring to step 2 of "Making Bias Tape" (page 9), use the striped pink 1" x 6" strips to make five ½"-wide tape pieces.

2. Thread a hand-sewing needle with a doubled strand of thread to match the pink fabric. Beginning at the upper-right corner of a tape piece, sew a running stitch that ends ½" from the lower-right corner. Stitch up to the top fold, creating an upside-down triangle with a 1"-wide base. Continue stitching the triangle pattern across the length of the strip, ending at the upper-left corner of the strip.

Mark the strip in 1" increments.

3. Pull the thread to gather the strip. Do not knot the thread. Bring the strip ends together and adjust the gathers to form a flower, tightening or loosening the gathers as needed. Whipstitch the raw ends of the strip together. On the back of the flower, zigzag stitch across the long raw edges to keep the edges from showing on the front of the flower if necessary; knot your thread on the back of the flower, but do not cut it. Whipstitch the petals together in the center of the flower; knot and cut your thread.

4. Repeat steps 2 and 3 to make a total of five flowers.

5. Cut the pink embellishing yarn into five 5"-long pieces. Wrap one piece of embellishing yarn around one finger three to four times, and then twist the loops into a figure-eight shape. Thread a hand-sewing needle with thread to match the pink embellishing yarn. Place the twisted loop of embellishing yarn on the center of one flower and stab stitch the center of the loops down to cover the flower center. Repeat for each flower.

6. Stab stitch three white drop beads in the center of each flower; knot the thread on the back of the flower.

making the stems and leaves

1. Referring to "Making Bias Tape" (page 9), use the green fabric to make 15" of ¼"-wide bias tape for the stems. Fold the bias tape in half to measure ⅛" wide; press.

2. Referring to the quilt photo (page 70) as needed, cut the bias-tape stems into five stems of varying length. Glue-baste the stems to the prepared background fabric, aligning one raw edge of each stem with the bottom raw edge of the quilt. Appliqué the stems in place.

3. Refer to "Basic Leaves" (page 10) to cut two 4½" x 10" strips from the remaining green fabric and make 14 leaves. Each leaf should measure ½" wide at the bottom and 2½" high. Cut out the leaves and turn them right side out, finger-pressing them into shape.

2½"

½" Raw edges

Make 14.

4. Glue-baste the bottom edge of the leaves to the bottom edge of the quilt, aligning the raw edges.

5. Referring to "Binding the Quilt" (page 8), use the striped pink 2½" x 42" strip to make the binding and finish the edges of the quilt. Make sure the raw edges of the leaves and stems are covered by the binding.

finishing

Refer to the quilt photo as needed.

1. Appliqué the flowers to the tops of the stems.

2. Referring to "Couching Threads for Embellishment" (page 15), couch the green embellishing yarn along the bottom of the stems to form the grass, leaving the ends to dangle for added texture.

3. Twist and turn the leaves as desired and tack them in place.

Real-life fuchsias look anything but simple, but these fabric versions really are easy to make. Colors can vary from bold orange to deep burgundy and from pure white to soft blue, so let your imagination run wild with color.

simple FUCHSIAS

materials

2 pieces, 9" x 7", of white tone-on-tone fabric for background and backing

1 strip, 2½" x 42", of green fabric for leaves and binding

1 strip, 1¾" x 42", of red fabric for flowers

1 strip, 1" x 42", of green fabric for calyxes

9" x 7" piece of thin, dense batting

Sewing thread to match fabrics

½ yard of green chenille yarn for stem

22" of black nylon rattail cord for flower stamens

22 red seed beads, size 10/0

Embellishing glue

making the quilt top

Unlike a standard appliqué quilt, this project requires that you quilt and bind the quilt before adding the appliquéd flowers. Work through the following steps, referring to "Basic Quilt Construction" (page 6) as needed.

1. Layer the backing, batting, and background pieces.

2. Baste and quilt the layers, and then square the quilt to 8" x 6".

3. Use the green 2½" x 42" strip to make the binding and finish the edges of the quilt. Save the remainder of the strip for making the leaves.

making the flowers

1. Layer the red 1¾" x 42" strip and the green 1" x 42" strip, right sides together, with one long, raw edge aligned. Stitch the strips together along the aligned edges. Press the seam allowance toward the red fabric. Crosscut the strip set into 11 segments, 2" wide.

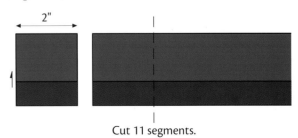

Cut 11 segments.

Finished size: 8" x 6"

2. Fold the segments in half, right sides together, so that the newly cut edges meet. Sew the cut edges together, using a ¼" seam allowance. Turn the segments right side out and finger-press the seam open. Turn under a scant ¼" hem around the green section of each segment and a ½" hem around the red section of each segment; finger-press the hems in place.

3. Cut the black embellishing thread into 11 pieces, 2" long. Use the embellishing glue to attach a red bead to both ends of each piece; allow the glue to dry. Make 11 stamen units.

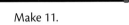

Make 11.

4. Thread a hand-sewing needle with thread to match the red fabric. Insert the needle into a flower segment at the seam, about ¼" from the bottom of the flower. Sew a running stitch all the way around the flower, making sure you are securing the hem as you sew. Fold one of the prepared stamen units in half and insert it into the center of the flower so that both seed beads are extending about ½" past the bottom of the flower. Pull the thread to tightly gather the flower around the stamens. Stitch through the flower and stamen unit several times to secure the thread unit in the flower and lock the flower shape; knot and cut the thread on the back (seam side) of the flower. Repeat for all 11 segments.

5. Thread a hand-sewing needle with thread to match the green fabric. Stitch a running stitch along the hemmed edge of the green fabric of a flower segment; pull the threads to tightly gather

the fabric to form the calyx. Knot the thread but don't cut it. Reinsert the needle into the seam between the red and green fabrics. Sew a running stitch around the flower, and then pull the thread to slightly gather the fabrics; knot the thread on the back (seam side) of the flower. Repeat with the remaining segments to make 11 flowers.

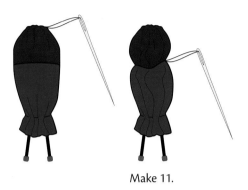

Make 11.

making the leaves

Referring to "Basic Leaves" (page 10), use the remainder of the green fabric to make 11 leaves. Each leaf should measure ½" wide at the bottom and 1½" high. Cut out the leaves and turn them right side out, finger-pressing them into shape. Turn up a ⅛" hem around the bottom of each leaf; finger-press it in place. Use matching green thread to tightly gather the bottom edge of each leaf.

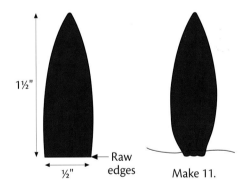

finishing

Refer to the quilt photo at left as needed.

1. Use the green chenille yarn to form the stem for the flowers. Referring to "Couching Threads for Embellishment" (page 15), couch the chenille yarn to the background fabric.

2. Appliqué the flowers to the chenille stem.

3. Appliqué the leaves to the chenille stem.

Finished size: 6½" x 8"

I have always loved fuchsias; they just seem like ballerinas dancing on the wind. I also love shopping the "sale" bins for bargain beads to add to my stash. I found the beads that I used for the stamens on these fuchsias a long time ago. When I was working on this quilt, I couldn't believe how wonderfully the beads went with the fabric. It was almost like I had a plan!

flared FUCHSIAS

materials

2 pieces, 7" x 9", of mottled yellow fabric for background and backing

1 strip, 2½" x 42", of mottled yellow fabric for binding

1 strip, 2¼" x 42", of multicolored fabric for flowers

1 strip, 1" x 42", of green fabric for calyxes

2 strips, 2" x 15", of dark green fabric for leaves

7" x 9" piece of thin, dense batting

Sewing thread to match fabrics

¾ yard of purple nylon rattail cord for flower stamens

¾ yard of yellow nylon rattail cord for flower stamens

½ yard of green chenille yarn for stem

24 multicolored seed beads, size 10/0

Embellishing glue

making the quilt top

Unlike a standard appliqué quilt, this project requires that you quilt and bind the quilt before adding the appliquéd flowers. Work through the following steps, referring to "Basic Quilt Construction" (page 6) as needed.

1. Layer the backing, batting, and background pieces.

2. Baste and quilt the layers, and then square the quilt to 6½" x 8".

3. Use the mottled yellow 2½" x 42" strip to make the binding and finish the edges of the quilt.

making the flowers

1. Layer the multicolored 2¼" x 42" strip and the green 1" x 42" strip right sides together, with one long, raw edge aligned. Stitch the strips together along the aligned edges. Press the seam allowance toward the multicolored fabric. Crosscut the strip set into eight segments, 3" wide.

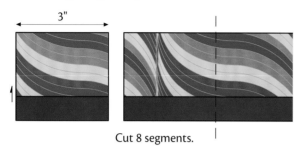

Cut 8 segments.

2. Fold the segments in half, right sides together, so that the newly cut edges meet. Sew the cut edges together, using a ¼" seam allowance. Turn the segments right side out and finger-press the seam allowance open. Turn under a scant ¼" hem around the green section of each segment and a ¾" hem around the multicolored section of each segment; finger-press the hems in place.

¾" hem
¼" hem

3. Cut the purple rattail cord into eight 3"-long pieces. Cut the yellow rattail cord into eight 2½"-long pieces. Use the embellishing glue to attach a bead to both ends of each purple piece and one end of each yellow piece; allow the glue to dry.

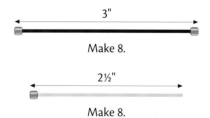

3"
Make 8.

2½"
Make 8.

4. Fold each purple cord from step 3 in half to find the center; crease the fold. Tie and knot a yellow piece to the center of each purple cord. Make eight stamen units.

Make 8.

5. Thread a hand-sewing needle with thread to match the green fabric; knot the ends together. Stitch a running stitch along the hemmed edge of the green fabric of a flower segment; pull the threads to tightly gather the fabric to form the calyx. Knot the thread but don't cut it. Reinsert the needle into the seam between the multicolored and green fabrics. Sew a running stitch around the flower, and then pull the thread to slightly gather the fabrics; knot the thread on the back (seam side) of the flower. Repeat with the remaining segments to make eight flowers.

6. Thread a hand-sewing needle with thread to match the multicolored fabric; knot the ends. Insert the needle into a flower segment at the seam, about ½" from the bottom of the flower. Sew a running stitch all the way around the flower, making sure you are securing the hem as you sew. Insert one of the prepared stamens at the center of the flower so that all three seed beads extend about ¾" past the bottom of the flower. Pull the thread to tightly gather the flower around the stamens. Stitch through the flower and stamen unit several times to secure the thread unit in the flower and lock

the flower shape; knot and cut the thread on the back (seam side) of the flower. Repeat for all eight segments.

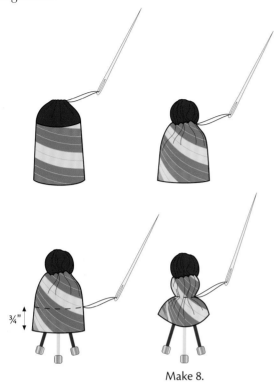

Make 8.

making the leaves

Referring to "Basic Leaves" (page 10), use the dark green 2" x 15" strips to make 24 leaves. Each leaf should measure ½" wide at the bottom and 1" high. Cut out the leaves and turn them right side out, finger-pressing them into shape. Turn under a ⅛" hem around the bottom of each leaf; finger-press it in place. Use matching green thread to tightly gather the bottom edge of each leaf.

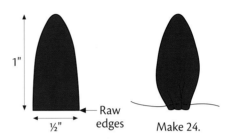

1"

½"

Raw edges

Make 24.

finishing

Refer to the quilt photo on page 76 as needed.

1. Referring to "Couching Thread for Embellishing" (page 15), couch the green chenille yarn to the background fabric to form the stem.

2. Appliqué the flowers to the chenille stem

3. Appliqué the leaves to the chenille stem.

Finished size: 7" x 10½"

This flower looks just like its name—a balloon! All puffed up and ready for a party, the balloon flower is super easy to make. The balloon flowers that grow in the real world are mostly shades of blue or white, but in my world they can be any color of the rainbow!

BALLOON
flowers

materials

2 pieces, 8" x 11", of white tone-on-tone fabric for background and backing

3 strips, 1¼" x 42", of mottled red fabric for flowers

3 strips, 1" x 42", of green fabric for calyxes

¼ yard of green fabric for stems and leaves

1 strip, 2½" x 42", of mottled red fabric for binding

8" x 11" piece of thin, dense batting

Sewing thread to match fabrics

1 yard of green embellishing yarn for grass

½ yard of variegated reddish orange embellishing yarn for grass accent

Water-soluble fabric glue

Template material

¼" bias-tape maker

making the quilt top

Unlike a standard appliqué quilt, this project requires that you quilt the quilt top before adding the appliquéd flowers. Work through the following steps, referring to "Basic Quilt Construction" (page 6) as needed.

1. Layer the backing, batting, and background pieces.

2. Baste and quilt the layers, and then square the quilt to 7" x 10½". Don't bind the quilt yet.

making the flowers

1. Layer a mottled red 1¼" x 42" strip and a green 1" x 42" strip right sides together, with one long, raw edge aligned. Stitch the strips together along the aligned edges. Press the seam allowance toward the red fabric. Repeat to make a total of three strip sets. Crosscut the strip sets into 31 segments, 3" wide.

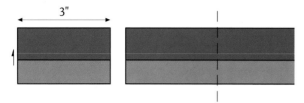

2. Fold each segment in half, right sides together, so that the newly cut edges meet. Sew the cut edges together, using a ¼" seam allowance. Turn the segments right side out and finger-press the seam allowance open.

3. Turn under a ⅛" hem around the green section of each segment; finger-press it in place. Thread a hand-sewing needle with thread to match the green fabric. Sew a running stitch along the folded edge and pull the thread tightly to gather. Knot the thread on the back (seam side) of the flower.

⅛" hem

4. Repeat step 3 on the red section of each segment, using thread that matches the red fabric, to complete each flower. Make 31 flowers.

⅛" hem

Make 31.

making the stems and leaves

1. Referring to "Making Bias Tape" (page 9), use the green fabric to make 40" of ¼"-wide bias tape.

Referring to the quilt photo (page 80), cut the strips into seven stems of varying lengths. Glue-baste the stems to the prepared background fabric, aligning one raw end of each stem with the bottom raw edge of the quilt. Appliqué the stems in place.

2. Referring to "Binding the Quilt" (page 8), use the mottled red 2½" x 42" strip to make the binding and finish the edges of the quilt. Make sure the raw edges of the stems are covered by the binding.

3. Use the leaf pattern below to make a template for the leaves from the template material. From the remainder of the green fabric, cut two 4" x 11" strips. Place the strips right sides together. Using the leaf template, trace nine leaves onto the layered strips, aligning the straight edge of the template with the raw edges of the fabric. Stitch around the curved edges. Cut out the leaves and turn them right side out, finger-pressing them into shape. Turn under a ¼" hem around the bottom of each leaf and finger-press it in place. Use matching green thread to tightly gather the bottom edge of each leaf.

finishing

Refer to the quilt photo as needed.

1. Appliqué the flowers to the stems with the seam side down.

2. Tack the leaves to the stems, adding tucks as desired.

3. Referring to "Couching Threads for Embellishment" (page 15), twist the green embellishing yarn with the reddish orange embellishing yarn and couch them to the bottom edge of the quilt to form the grass, leaving the ends to dangle for added texture.

Leaf
Make 9.

Hollyhocks are one of my favorite flowers. I am not able to grow them in my garden because of the tendency to develop rust, a fungal disease, so I decided to make my own bouquet of everlasting hollyhocks. These elegant, old-fashioned flowers exude warmth and classic cottage garden style.

holly HOCKS

materials

2 pieces, 13" x 13", of blue fabric for background and backing

1 strip, 3" x 42", of pink fabric for flowers

1 strip, 3" x 42", of orange fabric for flowers

1 strip, 3" x 42", of yellow fabric for flowers

¼ yard of green fabric for stems, leaves, and calyxes

2 strips, 2½" x 42", of pink fabric for binding

13" x 13" piece of thin, dense batting

Sewing thread to match fabrics

2 yards of pink embellishing yarn for flower centers

2 yards of orange embellishing yarn for flower centers

2½ yards of yellow embellishing yarn for flower centers

1 yard of green embellishing yarn for grass

1 yard of multicolored embellishing yarn for grass accent

140 pink seed beads, size 10/0

140 orange seed beads, size 10/0

175 light yellow seed beads, size 10/0

91 bright yellow seed beads, size 10/0

¼ yard of sewable fusible web

Water-soluble fabric glue

Template material

¼" bias-tape maker

Finished size: 12" x 12"

making the quilt top

Unlike a standard appliqué quilt, this project requires that you quilt the top before adding the appliquéd flowers. Work through the following steps, referring to "Basic Quilt Construction" (page 6) as needed.

1. Layer the backing, batting, and background pieces.

2. Baste and quilt the layers, and then square the quilt to 12" x 12". Don't bind the quilt yet.

making the flowers

1. Press under a ¼"-wide hem along both long sides of the pink, orange, and yellow 3" x 42" strips. Fold each of the strips in half lengthwise, wrong sides together; press. Each strip should now measure 1¼" x 42".

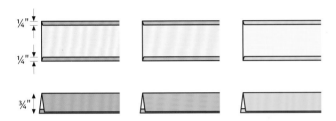

2. Crosscut the pink strip into three 6"-wide sections for the large flowers, one 5"-wide section for the medium flower, one 2"-wide section for the large bud, and two 1½"-wide sections for the small buds. Cut the orange strip into three 6"-wide sections for the large flowers, one 5"-wide section for the medium flower, and two 4"-wide sections for the buds. Cut the yellow strip into three 6"-wide sections for the large flowers, two 5"-wide sections for the medium flowers, and one 3"-wide section for the flower bud.

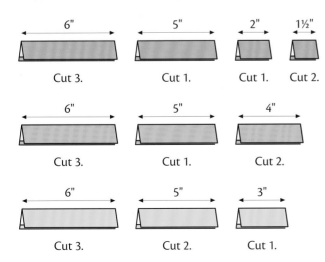

3. For *each* section from step 2, press under a ¼" hem on one cut edge. With right sides out, loop the raw edge of each strip around and into the finished edge of the strip. Use matching thread to blindstitch the seam.

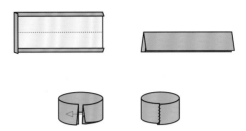

4. Use a long running stitch to gather the bottom edge of each piece tightly to form a cup shape. Pass the needle through the bottom edge several times to lock the shape; knot the thread.

5. Cut the pink and orange embellishing yarns each into four 18"-long pieces and the yellow embellishing yarn into five 14"-long pieces.

6. Wrap one piece of embellishing yarn around your finger 8 to 10 times, and then twist the loops into a figure-eight shape. Thread a hand-sewing needle with sewing thread to match the embellishing yarn. Place the twisted loop of embellishing yarn on the center of a matching large or medium flower piece and stab stitch the center of the loops down to cover the flower center. Knot the thread on the back of the flower, but do not cut it.

7. Bring the needle up from the bottom of the flower piece and thread five seed beads that match the flower (use light yellow beads for the yellow flowers) onto the needle. Add a bright yellow seed bead. Pass the threaded needle back through the five matching beads, and then reinsert the needle right next to the spot where it first emerged; knot the thread on the back of the flower, but do not cut it. Repeat the process until you have seven stamens in the center of the flower. (Knotting after each stack of beads keeps the beads tight against the flower, and if the thread breaks you will only have to rethread the last stack.)

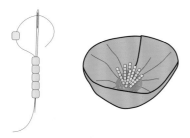

8. Repeat steps 6 and 7 for all the large and medium flower pieces.

making the stems

1. Referring to "Making Bias Tape" (page 9), use the green fabric to make three 10"-long pieces of ¼"-wide bias tape. Glue-baste the stems to the prepared background fabric, aligning one raw end of each stem with the bottom raw edge of the quilt. Appliqué the stems in place.

2. Referring to "Binding the Quilt" (page 8), use the pink 2½" x 42" strips to make the binding and finish the edges of the quilt. Make sure the raw edges of the stems are covered by the binding.

making the calyxes and flower buds

1. Referring to "Making a Calyx" (page 12), cut two 2" x 9" strips from the green fabric and make six calyxes for the flower buds. Each calyx should measure about ¾" wide at the bottom and ¾"

high. Cut out the calyxes and turn them right side out. Turn under a ⅛" hem around the bottom of each calyx; finger-press it in place.

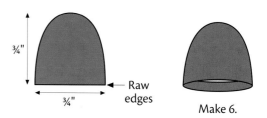

¾"

¾"

Raw edges

Make 6.

2. Insert a flower bud into each calyx, making sure all the raw edges of the flower bud are covered by the calyx. Using matching green thread, blindstitch the calyxes to the flower buds, pulling the thread slightly to gather. Stitch through the flower buds several times to lock the shape; knot the thread on the back of each bud. Make six flower buds.

Make 1.   Make 2.   Make 1 small and 2 extra-small.

making the leaves

1. Use the patterns at right to make templates for the large, medium, small, and extra-small leaves from the template material. Refer to "Fused Leaves" (page 11) and use the templates, the remainder of the green fabric, and the fusible web to make six large leaves, six medium leaves, six small leaves, and three extra-small leaves. Use matching green thread to topstitch the veins on each leaf, following the patterns. Zigzag stitch around the outer edge of each leaf. Cut out the leaves and then press each one to set the topstitching.

2. Refer to the quilt photo (page 84) to tack the leaves to the stems.

finishing

Refer to the quilt photo on page 84 as needed.

1. Appliqué the flowers and buds to the stems, placing the buds at the top of the stems, followed by the medium and then the large flowers.

2. Referring to "Couching Threads for Embellishment" (page 15), twist the multicolored embellishing yarn with the green embellishing yarn and couch them to the bottom edge of the quilt to form the grass, leaving the ends to dangle for added texture.

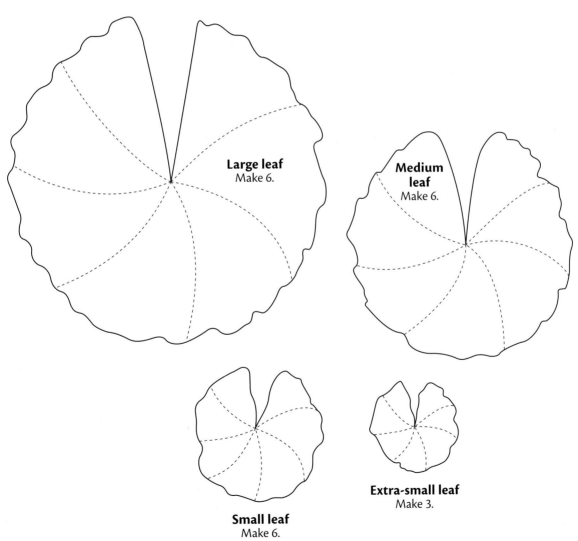

Large leaf
Make 6.

Medium leaf
Make 6.

Small leaf
Make 6.

Extra-small leaf
Make 3.

Finished size: 10" x 12½"

It is so unusual to see a green flower! I fell in love with the Bells of Ireland as soon as I saw them. The green part of the flower is the calyx and the white petals in the center are really the flower.

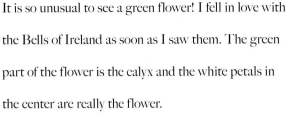

bells of
IRELAND

materials

2 pieces, 11" x 13½", of mottled blue fabric for background and backing

5 strips, 2" x 42", of mottled green fabric for flowers

⅓ yard of light green fabric for accent trim, leaves, and stems

1 strip, 2½" x 42", of mottled green fabric for binding

11" x 13½" piece of thin, dense batting

Sewing thread to match fabrics

1 yard of green embellishing yarn

52 small white flower-shaped beads

64 bright green seed beads, size 10/0

¼ yard of sewable fusible web

Water-soluble fabric glue

Template material

¼" bias-tape maker

making the quilt top

Unlike a standard appliqué quilt, this project requires that you quilt the quilt before adding the appliquéd flowers. Work through the following steps, referring to "Basic Quilt Construction" (page 6) as needed.

1. Layer the backing, batting, and background pieces.

2. Baste and quilt the layers, and then square the quilt to 10" x 12½". Don't bind the quilt yet.

making the flowers

1. Press under a ¼"-wide hem down both long sides of each mottled green 2" x 42" strip. Fold each of the strips in half lengthwise, wrong sides together; press. The strips should now measure ¾" x 42".

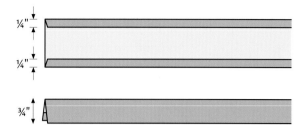

2. Crosscut three strips into 30 segments, 4" wide, for the large flowers. Crosscut one strip into 12 segments, 3¼" wide, for the medium flowers. Crosscut the remaining strip into 10 segments, 2" wide, for the small flowers.

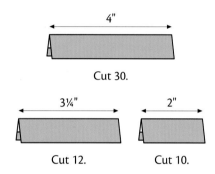

Cut 30.

Cut 12.   Cut 10.

3. For *each* segment from step 2, press under a ¼" hem on one cut edge. With right sides out, loop the raw edge of each strip around and into the finished edge of the strip. Use matching thread to blindstitch the seam.

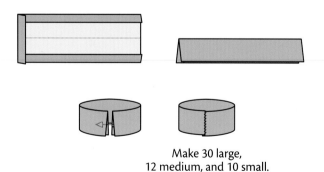

Make 30 large,
12 medium, and 10 small.

4. Use a running stitch to gather the bottom edge of each piece tightly to form a cup shape. Pass the needle through the bottom edge several times to lock the shape; knot the thread.

making the stems and leaves

1. Referring to "Making Bias Tape" (page 9), use the light green fabric to make 72" of ¼"-wide bias tape. Refer to the quilt photo (page 88) to cut the strips into seven stems of varying lengths. Glue-baste the stems to the prepared background fabric, aligning one raw end of each stem with the bottom raw edge of the quilt. Appliqué the stems in place.

2. Cut four 1" x 15" strips from the remainder of the light green fabric. Referring to "Adding Accent Trim" (page 7), add the accent strips to the quilt. Referring to "Binding the Quilt (page 8), use the mottled green 2½" x 42" strip to make the binding and finish the edges of the quilt. Make sure the raw edges of the stems are covered by the binding.

3. Use the patterns at right to make templates for the large, medium, and small leaves from the template material. Referring to "Fused Leaves" (page 11), use the templates, the remainder of the light green fabric, and the fusible web to make six large leaves, six medium leaves, and five small leaves. Use matching green thread to topstitch the center and side veins on each leaf, following the patterns. Zigzag stitch around the outer edge of each leaf. Cut out the leaves and then press each one to set the topstitching.

finishing

Refer to the quilt photo on page 88 as needed.

1. Tack the leaves to the stems.

2. Thread a hand-sewing needle with thread to match the green fabric. Bring the needle up through the center of the flower. Add a white flower bead and a green seed bead to the needle and stab stitch them in place. Knot the thread on the back of the flower, but do not cut it. Use the same thread to appliqué the flower to one of the stems. Repeat to add the large flowers first, and then work your way up the stem to the small flowers. Tuck the flowers tight against each other to make the flower stalk look full.

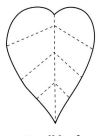

3. Use the bud pattern at right to make a template from the template material. Use the template to cut 12 buds from the remainder of the mottled green fabric. Refer to "Raw Edged Yo-Yos" (page 15) to make 12 raw-edged yo-yos.

4. Stab stitch one green seed bead in the center of a bud; knot the thread, but do not cut it. Use the same thread to appliqué the bud to the top of a stem. Repeat to add two buds to the top of each stem.

5. Referring to "Couching Threads for Embellishment" (page 15), use the green embellishing yarn to make the swirled foliage at the bottom of the quilt. Couch the yarns in place.

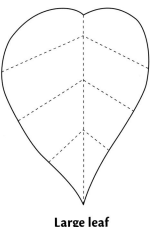

Large leaf
Make 6.

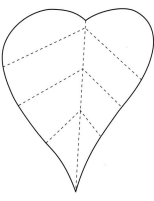

Medium leaf
Make 6.

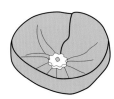

Small leaf
Make 5.

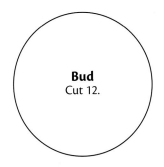

Bud
Cut 12.

gallery of QUILTS

Adding dimensional flowers to your quilt can make any project fabulous. All the quilts shown here in the gallery were created using the flowers in this book.

MINI TWO-COLOR SIX-PETAL FLOWERS

5" x 3¾"

Two colors of fabric are folded into prairie points and joined to form these mini flowers. Sparkly yarn in the center of each flower makes them a real showstopper!

MINI THREE-PETAL FLOWERS

5" x 3¾"

White prairie point flowers with pink stamens seem to glow on the blue background. Smaller red prairie point flowers, each with a single bead in the center, mingle at the base.

THREE-PETAL DROP FLOWERS

3¾" x 5"

These flowers are drop-dead gorgeous! Pink prairie points were joined to form the elegant, vibrant blooms.

THREE-PETAL CONEFLOWERS

3¾" x 5"

I love coneflowers! The bright pink centers of these flowers were made using hump-shaped pieces, which were then surrounded by white prairie points. A black embellishing thread separates the petals and centers. Any color combination will work for this flower.

FIESTA

5½" x 10½"

Hot, hot, hot! Fiery orange fabric was ruched to form flowers with a south-of-the-border feel. Stuffed leaves stand out against the dark, subtle background.

KOI POND

10½" x 11"

Fish were cut from a printed fabric and appliquéd in place to "swim" on a blue background. Green lily pads and a lone flower seem to float serenely on the pond's surface, giving a sense of tranquility. Instructions for a similar quilt are provided on page 49.

BIRDS OF A FEATHER

9" x 12½"

Birds of a feather always flock together! I thought a pair of bird quilts would be fun to hang side by side so it would look like they were talking to each other. The birds were fussy cut from an allover print fabric, and then the colors of their feathers were worked into the flowers. I think the results are fabulous.

CHERRY BLOSSOMS

8" x 11½"

This charming duo came about when I was given a small scrap of fabric and challenged to come up with some kind of quilt. Because I had to use it all, I decided to make two small wall quilts. The print reminded me of an old china pattern and I immediately thought of cherry blossoms. Simple raw-edged yo-yos and a dash of pink in the center bring these sweet springtime blossoms to life.

SUMMER PICNIC

15½" x 20"

Who doesn't love a picnic, or at least the thought of a picnic? I found this print and thought about how best to use it. The plump grapes are made with stuffed raw-edged yo-yos and the leaves are fused. This was one of the simplest projects I have ever done, but I love the way it turned out.

BLACK BEAUTIES

7" x 7"

Black flowers can be fabulous, too! Even the butterflies are attracted to this little quilt.

RESOURCES

FOR A WONDERFUL SELECTION OF BEADS:

Shipwreck Beads
8560 Commerce Place Dr. NE
Lacey, WA 98516
1-800-950-4232
www.shipwreckbeads.com

**FOR A WIDE RANGE OF EMBELLISHING
THREADS AND YARNS:**

Rainbow Gallery
7412 Fulton Ave., No. 5
North Hollywood, CA 91605
www.rainbowgallery.com

Rainbow Gallery doesn't offer mail order, but the
company will direct you to stores in your area that
carry its products.

Fabulous Fibers
PO Box 158
Lyndora, PA 16045
724-355-5050
www.fabulousfibers.com

FOR KAI SCISSORS:

Shear Precision Scissor Co.
PO Box 13671
Seattle, WA 98198-1009
1-800-481-4943
www.kaiscissors.com

ABOUT THE author

Sharon Baker loves all forms of arts and crafts, but her love of quilting outshines them all. Creating realistic three-dimensional flowers from fabric to incorporate into her quilts has become a driving passion in recent years. Having been born blind in her right eye, she sees the world in a very flat way, so she likes to incorporate some kind of three-dimensional element into her work. She shared many of her earlier quilt creations in her first book, *Fabulous Flowers: Mini-Quilts in Dimensional Appliqué* (Martingale & Company, 2005).

When she isn't quilting, Sharon enjoys spending hours in her garden studying the complexities of nature, communing with nature as she four-wheels, baking bread, making jams and jellies, and spending time with her husband and two sons, who thankfully, she says, are accustomed to her obsessive behavior and passion for fabric, beads, and embellishing threads.

For workshop and lecture information, contact Sharon at ohsewcrazyone@msn.com.